CALIFORNIA

Doris Day's Cypress Inn in Carmel.

BED AND BREAKFAST GUIDES

CALIFORNIA

SOUTHERN CALIFORNIA, CENTRAL COAST, SAN FRANCISCO
AND THE BAY AREA, GOLD COUNTRY, WINE COUNTRY,
NORTHERN CALIFORNIA

BY LUCY POSHEK, NAOMI BLACK, TERRY BERGER,
AND COURTIA WORTH

Photographs by Lucy Poshek, Will Faller,
and Jeanne Somers

DESIGNED AND PRODUCED BY
ROBERT R. REID AND TERRY BERGER

MACMILLAN • USA

Front cover: *a guest room at the Blue Lantern Inn, Dana Point.*
Back cover: *photographs of the Captain Walsh House, Benicia.*
Frontispiece: *the ocean beach at St. Orres, near Gualala on the North Coast.*

Published by Macmillan Travel
A Prentice Hall Macmillan Company
15 Columbus Circle
New York, NY 10023

MACMILLAN is a registered trademark of Macmillian, Inc.

Library of Congress Card No. 1084-0567
ISBN 0-02-860879-8

_____

A Robert Reid Associates production
Typeset in Bodoni Book by Monotype Composition Company, Baltimore
Produced by Mandarin Offset, Hong Kong
Printed in Hong Kong

1 2 3 4 5 6 7 8 9 10

CONTENTS

continued overleaf

NORTHERN CALIFORNIA

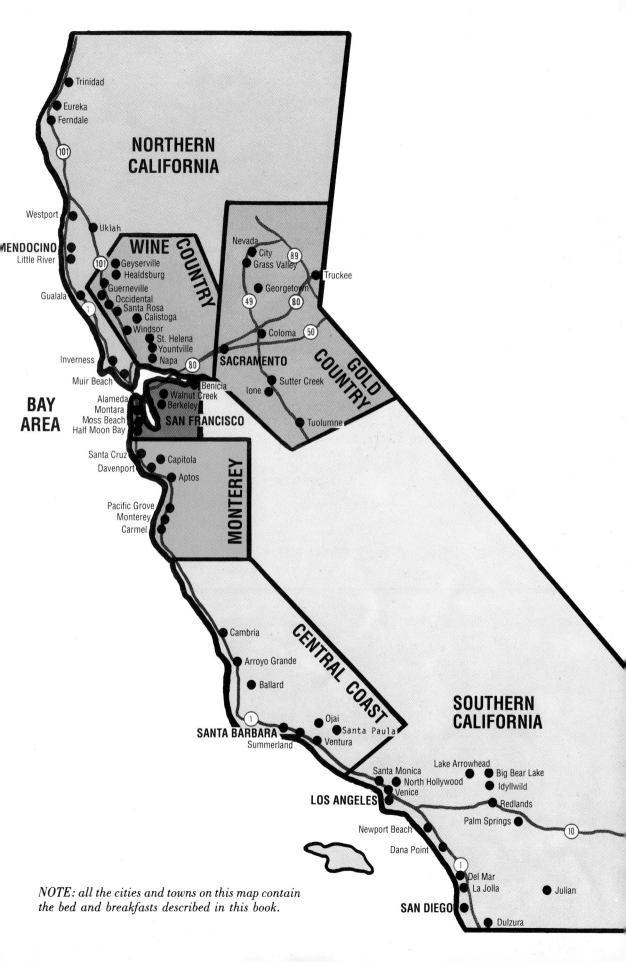

Trinidad
Eureka
Ferndale

**NORTHERN
CALIFORNIA**

101

Westport
Ukiah
MENDOCINO
Little River

WINE COUNTRY

101
Geyserville
Healdsburg
Gualala
Guerneville
Occidental
Santa Rosa
Calistoga
1
Windsor
St. Helena
Yountville
Inverness
Napa
80

Nevada
City
Grass Valley
89
Truckee
Georgetown
49
80
Coloma
50

SACRAMENTO

GOLD COUNTRY

Muir Beach
Benicia
Walnut Creek
Sutter Creek
Ione
Alameda
Berkeley
Montara
Moss Beach
SAN FRANCISCO
Tuolumne
Half Moon Bay

**BAY
AREA**

Santa Cruz
Davenport
Capitola
Aptos

MONTEREY

Pacific Grove
Monterey
Carmel

Cambria

CENTRAL COAST

Arroyo Grande

Ballard

**SOUTHERN
CALIFORNIA**

1
Ojai
Santa Paula
SANTA BARBARA
Ventura
Summerland

Santa Monica
Lake Arrowhead
Big Bear Lake
North Hollywood
Idyllwild
Venice
Redlands
LOS ANGELES
Palm Springs
Newport Beach
10
Dana Point
1
Del Mar
La Jolla
Julian
SAN DIEGO
Dulzura

*NOTE: all the cities and towns on this map contain
the bed and breakfasts described in this book.*

SOUTHERN CALIFORNIA

ORCHARD HILL

Craftsman-style hospitality

Orchard Hill Country Inn is set on a rise just above historic downtown Julian, with its turn-of-the-century storefronts. Lined by fragrant banks of rosemary, the driveway leads up to a row of newly built Craftsman-style cottages, each containing three suites. Further up the hill is the main lodge where a dining room, library-conference room, more guest quarters, and a high-ceilinged gathering area are located.

Whereas the bedrooms in the main lodge have the best view of Julian, the cottage suites are the most luxurious. Handsomely appointed in fresh country themes by owner and interior designer Pat Straube, most of the suites feature high, vaulted ceilings, fireplaces (some double-sided), sitting areas, wet bars, televisions, VCR's (with scads of videos available), and large, pristine bathrooms with whirlpool tubs for two. Sweet Bough, Cortland, Roxbury and

Left, a garden cottage.

The breakfast-eye view of Julian.

Bell Flower are among the favorite suites.

Everything is done well at Orchard Hill, from the welcoming staff to the thoughtful extras. In addition to the usual room amenities guests will find a basket of games, knitted slippers, and an extra quilt for those frosty mountain nights. Cookies are brought to your room upon arrival. In the early evening, a plate of hot hors d'oeuvres and a split of locally-made wine are delivered. In the morning, guests can select from among a wide range of breakfast items in the main lodge. From here, downtown Julian is only two blocks away.

ORCHARD HILL COUNTRY INN, 2502 Washington St., PO Box 425, Julian, CA 92036-0425; (619) 765-1700; Fax (619) 765-0290; Darrell & Pat Straube, owners. Closed 2 weeks in January. Twelve suites in four cottages and ten rooms in main lodge, all with private baths; some rooms custom-designed for the physically challenged. Rates: $130 to $155, including full breakfast and afternoon hors d'oeuvres. Children welcome; smoking allowed outdoors only; no pets; Visa/MasterCard/American Express. Historic walks, mine tours, wineries, shopping, and carriage rides nearby. Orchard Hill Country Inn, Pine Hills Dinner Theatre and Julian Grille recommended for dining.

DIRECTIONS: entering downtown Julian from SR-78/79 east, cross Main St. to Washington St. and go 2 blocks north.

The Roxbury Room.

Hosts Jim and Loretta Ketcherside at one of their guest houses, the Enchanted Cottage, whose charm is enhanced by a wood-burning stove.

The Tree House is only eleven steps off the ground, but, with the feather beds, it feels like heaven.

SHADOW MOUNTAIN RANCH

"We like to live our fantasies"

When Jim and Loretta Ketcherside retired from working in the school system, they generously offered a foreign visitor a place to stay for the night. "We hadn't planned to have a B&B," remarked Loretta. But they soon began transforming their predominantly cedar ranch house into a bed and breakfast with a unique personality.

The pastoral setting on eight acres allowed the Ketchersides to build separate guest cottages in addition to the rooms in the main house. Gramma's Attic features a plump feather bed, cream and white bed linens, and in one corner, Loretta's satin wedding dress. The Enchanted Cottage resembles a Disneyesque Bavarian bungalow with arched doorway, green and peach décor, and a lovely bay windowseat. Still, the favorite room, even for guests who opt not to stay there, is the treehouse. Perched above the deck, high in the branches, sits a wonderful, whimsical hideaway built around the tree trunk.

"We like to live our fantasies," says Jim, who constructed a secret passage from the hot tub to the Pine Room and who always wanted to try his hand at archery. Besides bows and arrows, guests here will find a manicured croquet/badminton lawn, a landscaped horseshoe pit, forty-foot lap pool, indoor hot tub, pool table, and fishing hole stocked with bluegill and bass.

SHADOW MOUNTAIN RANCH, Box 791, 2771 Frisius Rd., Julian, CA 92036; (619) 765-0323; Jim and Loretta Ketcherside, owners. Two rooms in main house, one with private bath; three cottage rooms with private baths, two-bedroom cottage, and a whimsical treehouse room. Rates: $80 to $100. Includes a full ranch breakfast and afternoon tea. No children under 18; no smoking permitted indoors; no pets. One Queensland heeler in residence. Facilities on premises: 40-ft. lap pool, indoor hot tub, teepee, archery, badminton, croquet, horseshoes, and catch-and-release fishing.

DIRECTIONS: from L.A. Take I-5 to Rte. 78 through Escondido. One mile before Julian there is a Methodist Church on the left and a sign for Pine Hills Lodge. Turn right onto Pine Hills Road. Go 2½ miles and take a left onto Frisius Road; entrance to the ranch is on the right. From San Diego take I-8 to Rte. 79 north through Julian one mile to the Methodist Church as above.

The extraordinary Victorian parlor.

HERITAGE PARK B&B INN

In the heart of Old Town

The most historic part of San Diego, popularly known as Old Town, was claimed for the King of Spain in 1769. Old Town's famous Presidio Park Plaza, Adobe Chapel, and other historic buildings are adjacent to a seven-acre hillside preserve called Heritage Park Victorian Village. Numerous Victorian houses were moved here when threatened with demolition.

One of the preserved homes, now Heritage Park Bed and Breakfast Inn, was literally cut in half and rejoined at its present site. It is an 1889 Queen Anne, characterized by a two-story corner tower, encircling veranda, and gingerbread fretwork.

The interior is filled with redwood trim, stained glass, and gaslight fixtures. The décor is very Victorian, with oriental rugs over wood floors, claw-foot tubs, and old-fashioned wall coverings.

HERITAGE PARK, 2470 Heritage Park Row, San Diego, CA 92110; (619) 295-7088, (800) 995-2470, Fax (619) 299-9465; Nancy and Charles Helsper, owners. Ten rooms, including one 2-room suite, all with private baths. Rates: $90 to $150 (suite $225); includes elaborate breakfast served in dining room. Turn down service and chocolate mints on each pillow. No pets; children allowed; smoking on the veranda; handicap access and accommodations; Christmas tours of the house; MasterCard/Visa.

DIRECTIONS: from downtown and airport: I-5 north to Old Town Avenue off-ramp. Left on Old Town Avenue, right on Harney to Heritage Park. From LA: I-5 to Old Town Avenue off-ramp, left on San Diego Avenue, and right on Harney.

BROOKSIDE FARM

Ten miles from Mexico

Brookside Farm offers the quaint pleasure of fetching brown eggs for breakfast from the Guishard's cooperative chickens, as well as a dramatic three-level terrace that is the gathering place for guests from morning coffee to late afternoon, under the shade of an ancient and gigantic California live oak.

Closest to the brook, on the third tier of the terrace are two guest rooms, The Wash House and The Wine Cellar, which are more rustic than the romantic Rose Room on the second floor, with its thick pink carpet, lace tablecloths, rose colored wallpaper, and panoramic view of the mountains. The Attic Room, with its oak rocker and original linoleum floor, has the finest view of the brook, and the brightest room, The Sun Room, is just off the dining room.

The living room is fronted with a bank of windows accented with royal blue stained glass made by Edd. The earth-colored Tecate Brick floor (made in Mexico just thirty miles to the south) and wood stove all add to the homey feel of this rural retreat.

BROOKSIDE FARM, 1373 Marron Valley Road, Dulzura, CA 92017; (619) 468-3043; Edd and Sally Guishard, hosts. Ten rooms, all with private baths. Rates: $75 to $115. Includes full varied breakfast such as California omelets with Ortega peppers and homemade biscuits, or blueberry pancakes with homemade sausage (exceptional!). Country Fare buffet often served on Sundays. Gourmet home-style dinner by reservation. Country Weekend, $195 to $275, includes breakfast and dinners. Complimentary light fare dinner Monday to Friday. No children; no pets; guests may smoke in designated areas; Visa/MasterCard/American Express/Discover.

DIRECTIONS: from San Diego: follow Rte. 94 to Dulzura; 1½ miles past Dulzura Café, right on Marron Valley Road.

The Sun Room.

The bungalow overlooks town and tides.

ROCK HAUS

Spectacular sunsets

As soon as you step onto the enclosed veranda and take in its panoramic view of the ocean, you'll know you have stopped at a special place. Rock Haus is inviting for breakfast and awesome at sunset, and the day can be spent walking on the beach, browsing through the fancy shops, or cheering on your favorite thoroughbred at the Del Mar Racetrack.

This landmark 1910 bungalow-style house has a large and welcoming living room, and rooms named Whale Watch, Wicker Garden, and Court Room, among others, have been meticulously decorated, each with individual charm and character.

ROCK HAUS, 410 15th Street, Del Mar, CA 92014; (619) 481-3764; Doris Holmes, host. Ten rooms, four with private baths and two with private entry on ground floor. Rates: $90 to $150. Includes continental breakfast. All major credit cards except American Express; children welcome; no pets; no smoking. Situated in the heart of Del Mar village; shops and beach are just a short walk away.

DIRECTIONS: from I-5 exit at Via de la Valle and head west to Jimmy Durante Blvd. Take a left and feed into US-101. Take a left on 15th Street.

Peace and tranquility.

THE B&B INN AT LA JOLLA

Steps away from seaside and shopping

With its air of sophistication and gentility, this fine bed and breakfast is perfectly suited to La Jolla. Artfully designed arches provide an entry to the house and gardens. The mood is so serene it is difficult to imagine that it is located on the periphery of the bustle of La Jolla's fancy shops and gourmet restaurants.

Special attention has gone into decorating the rooms. Each has a distinctive personality and flavor. Horizon, the master suite at the front of the house, is bright and spacious. Tall windows, a fireplace, a four-poster canopied bed, white couch and wing chairs add elegance and warmth. The Cove, with a more casual feeling, has warm peach walls, white wicker furniture, and a salmon and blue Dhurrie rug. Branches of trees can be seen blooming outside in the courtyard. Altogether different, and slightly masculine in tone, the Garden Room opens onto the courtyard. Although the walls are pale lavender, the hunter green

plaid wool comforter, handsomely painted rural folk art over the mantel, and rustic fireplace combine to make this room more like a den.

The Irving Gill Penthouse features a separate living room and an open sun deck, which in addition to the window seat and couch in the bedroom, lends itself to small entertaining.

For the pleasure of all the guests, there is a sitting room on the second floor of the original house which is vibrant during the day with its cool white walls and lavender accents. Tall arched windows welcome Southern California sun and a deck off the sitting room draws sun worshippers. The sitting room serves guests well in the evening too, whether it is to watch a bit of news on television or step out on the deck to gaze at the stars.

THE BED & BREAKFAST INN AT LA JOLLA, 7753 Draper Avenue, La Jolla, CA 92037; (619) 456-2066; Jeris Hackl, innkeeper. Sixteen charming rooms, 15 with private baths, several with sea view and fireplaces. Rates: $85 to $225 plus tax. Includes a continental-plus breakfast delivered to your room or served in the dining room, garden, or sundeck. Tennis courts 100 feet away. La Jolla Museum of Art across the street and shops and ocean less than a minute's walk. No pets; Visa/MasterCard.

DIRECTIONS: from the north or south: from I-5 take La Jolla Village Drive west. Left onto Torrey Pines Road for 3 miles and turn right onto Prospect Place. Go 10 blocks and bear left onto Draper Avenue across from Museum.

BLUE LANTERN INN

Perched high on a bluff

This grey, Cape Cod-style inn is perched high on a bluff above Dana Point Marina. Built in 1990, it is operated by the Four Sisters Inns, a fine collection of family-owned B&B's.

Each of the twenty-nine guest rooms at the Blue Lantern Inn have a different lay-out and are decorated in soft blues, lavenders, and greens. They all boast fireplaces, Jacuzzi tubs, and antique reproduction furnishings. Those rooms facing the sea have the most fantastic view overlooking the pretty harbor and hundreds of boats. The third-floor Tower Suite is particularly striking with its high vaulted ceiling and ocean panorama.

Blue Lantern runs with the smooth efficiency of a hotel, but the personal touches keep it from being too much like one. Stuffed bears—a Four Sisters trademark—are not only gathered in amusing positions around the lounge and fireplace, but in each guest room, as well. Homebaked chocolate chip cookies, fruit and beverages are available throughout the day. Afternoon tea with wine, hors d'oeuvres, and a sweet are served either in the sunroom or library. The country breakfast buffet might include such treats as French bread custard and cinnamon coffee. The morning paper, evening turndown, use of the inn's bicycles and exercise room are among the other extras provided.

Dana Point Marina offers a wide range of restaurants and activities, while just ten minutes up the coast is Laguna Beach, with its stunning beaches, unique shops, and galleries.

Left above, a view of Dana Point harbor from a guest room, showing the beach. Below, The guest rooms have wonderful views of the Pacific.

BLUE LANTERN INN, 34343 Street of the Blue Lantern, Dana Point, CA 92629; (800) 950-1236; (714) 661-1304; Fax (714) 496-1483; Nancy Teel, manager. Open all year. Twenty-nine rooms and suites, all with private baths, Jacuzzi tubs and fireplaces. Rates: $135 to $350, including full country breakfast and afternoon wine, tea, and hors d'oeuvres. Children welcome; no smoking; no pets; Visa/MasterCard/American Express. Whale watching (in season), golf, boating, beaches, and Mission San Juan Capistrano nearby. Cannons, Lucianos, and Charthouse recommended for dining.

DIRECTIONS: from Hwy. 1 in Dana Point, turn west on Street of the Blue Lantern and proceed one block.

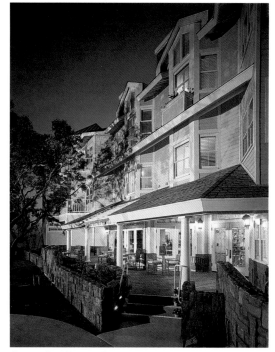

The inn building and inviting patio.

The salon/lobby off the patio.

DORYMAN'S INN

Total luxury
at Newport Beach

It is immediately apparent that no expense or comfort was spared in the execution of this extraordinary bed and breakfast. As you step off the street into a small vestibule, a receding oak door exposes an expansive gold-leafed mirror, luminous brass railing, quartersawed wainscoting, silk wallpaper, and rich wool carpeting. You have just stepped into the elevator at Doryman's Inn.

Upon arriving at the second floor, you are ushered along a skylighted hallway to one of the opulent rooms. Appointments include Italian mar-

ble fireplaces, luxurious window seats, antique furnishings, and artwork collected from all over the world.

The effort to please is apparent, whether you take the celebrity suite facing the ocean, with the sitting area, four-poster, conference table, and marble Jacuzzi, or the room with the ocean view and the rosette-pleated canopy. One-way glass has been installed in all of the windows to ensure total privacy, walls are insulated, and doors are two-and-a-half-inches of solid oak. Bedside controls raise or lower gas-fueled fireplaces that glow in all the rooms, and each of the marble bathrooms has a fern-filled skylight, sunken tub, and telephone.

A buffet-style full breakfast is served in the parlor and may be eaten there or elsewhere. Other features of this 1921 landmark building include a redwood sun deck and Jacuzzi for eight on top of the complex, and Rex's fine restaurant on the ground floor. As if that weren't enough, Doryman's is located right at the beach and boardwalk of Newport Pier.

DORYMAN'S INN. 2102 W. Ocean Front, Newport Beach, CA 92663; (714) 675-7300; Michael Palitz, owner. French and Italian spoken. Ten rooms, six with ocean views, all with private baths, including two Jacuzzis. Rates: $135 to $275. Includes an expanded continental breakfast. Ground floor restaurant caters to rooms; limo service to and from airport. Children welcome; no pets; Visa/MasterCard/American Express.

DIRECTIONS: located at the base of Newport Pier.

The romance of the inn comes alive at night.

VILLA ROYALE

An elegant garden paradise

Elvis, Marilyn Monroe, Frank Sinatra, Elizabeth Taylor—all have called Palm Springs home at one time or another. Villa Royale owner Bob Lee credits Palm Springs' fame to this fact and its "guaranteed perfect weather." Rimmed by mountains on all four sides, this desert oasis is host to an international film festival, indoor polo, the country's largest man-made surf pool, and "more golf courses than anywhere else in the world."

It's the ideal setting for Bob's distinctive bed-and-breakfast resort. This innovative host created areas in which guests can disappear to be alone. Private patios, a gazebo, an outdoor living room, even secluded spas, are the order of the day here. Spread out over three and-a-half acres, each of the thirty-one ground-floor rooms summons the atmosphere of a particular country. Fishing nets adorn the walls of the Algarve; a cuckoo clock and beer steins recall Bavaria; while a leather-upholstered chair and an antique wooden cupboard evoke the flavor of Spain.

A fabulous restaurant à la Northern Italian style features continental cuisine including roast duck with caramelized orange, rack of lamb, and salmon with mushrooms, zucchini, and crème fraîche baked in parchment.

For eleven years little has changed here; it is still a haven from the work-weary world. Why tinker with an elegant garden paradise that works?

VILLA ROYALE, 1620 South Indian Trail, Palm Springs, CA 92264, (800) 245-2314, (619) 327-2314, Fax (619) 322-3794; Bob Lee, owner. Thirty-one rooms with private baths, most with private deck, terrace, or courtyard; many with fireplaces; some with private outdoor Jacuzzis. Telephone and disguised televisions in rooms. Rates: $65 to $295, additional person $25 per night. Summer discount rates. Includes continental breakfast. Adults preferred; no pets; smoking permitted; American Express/MasterCard/Visa/Diners Club; French, Spanish, and a little German spoken. Two swimming pools, whirlpool spa, VCRs.

DIRECTIONS: take I-10 to the Palm Springs exit. Continue on Palm Canyon Dr. until it turns into East Palm Canyon Drive, then take a left onto Indian Trail.

KORAKIA PENSIONE

Moroccan-style 1920s villa

Korakia Pensione is an exciting departure from the traditional B&B. The whitewashed, Moroccan-style villa was built in 1924 by a Scottish painter who spent much time in Tangiers. During the 20s and 30s the Palm Springs villa was a popular gathering spot for artists and writers. After suffering decades of decline, the building was purchased by Doug Smith, an architectural preservationist, who spent three years on its restoration.

While its castle-like turrets and whimsical archways are reminiscent of North Africa, other details of Korakia reflect Doug's love of Greece where he once lived. The exotic atmosphere extends inside, where one finds lofty ceilings, an array of Turkish carpets over tile floors, Moroccan bird cages, and rich fabrics contrasting dramatically with simple, white muslins.

The Library is one of the most inviting guest rooms. Once used for literary discussions and chamber music, this room features a heavy wood beamed ceiling, four-poster bed, fireplace, Oriental rugs over terra cotta floors, and bookshelves filled with rare books. Whereas the Library is exotically cozy, the upstairs Artist Studio (where Winston Churchill once painted) is light and airy, its large picture window and telescope facing the San Jacinto mountains.

This inn has become a hot new getaway spot for celebrities (among them, Peter Coyote and Ted Danson), and it's easy to see why. It blends a Mediterranean ambience with California-style informality. Guests are free to use the communal kitchen, rules

The Artist's Studio guest room.

are loose, and activities almost nill. The number-one pastime at Korakia is lounging around the pool under the hot desert sun.

KORAKIA PENSIONE, 257 S. Patencio Rd., Palm Springs, CA 92262; (619) 864-6411; G. Douglas Smith, owner. Closed August. Twelve rooms, all with private baths. Rates: $79 to $169, including continental breakfast. Inquire about children; smoking allowed; no pets; no credit cards. Indian canyons, tramway, great hiking, and Living Desert Reserve nearby. Cafe Saint James, Palmie and Doug Arangos recommended for dining.

DIRECTIONS: from SR-111 (Palm Canyon Dr.) south, turn right on Arenas Rd., then left on Patencio Rd.

STRAWBERRY CREEK INN

A cedar-shingled mountain inn

Originally called Strawberry Valley, Idyllwild flourished with an abundance of wild strawberries. When in 1901 a group of doctors bought much of the land for a tuberculosis sanitarium, they changed the town's name to Idyllwild, not inappropriate because of its location in San Bernadino National Forest.

Not far from the ranger station, at the center of this rural mountain community, stands a rambling cedar-shingled mountain house with wide picture windows and an unfailing ability to charm. Owners Diana Dugan and Jim Goff, both professional urban planners, left San Diego for a quieter life in the country.

Jim cooks up the scrumptious breakfasts—which range from German French toast with local sausage to sour cream-bacon omelets to spinach-zucchini quiche—while Diana tends to the crisp, neat, and picturesque rooms. Antiques, handmade quilts, and lots of inviting pillows give the rooms a special, cozy allure that makes many guests want to extend their stays.

Four additional rooms, arranged in a semicircle around a bleached wooden deck, form the Courtyard. The Santa Fe Room pays homage to the Southwest, with walls made to resemble stucco and dark wooden beams that stretch across the ceiling; the San Jacinto Room draws on the décor of an old mountain lodge with a red, white, and blue twist; while Helen's Room and the Autumn Room perfectly capture the feel of an airy Victorian boudoir and an American country bedchamber, respectively.

Strawberry Creek's common rooms enhance the already wonderful bedrooms. The comfortable couches and color-coordinated appointments, matched with the spaciousness and friendliness of the huge living room, make this a place in which to sit back, breathe deeply, and relax.

STRAWBERRY CREEK INN, 26370 Highway 243, P.O. Box 1818, Idyllwild, CA 92549; (909) 659-3202; Diana Dugan and Jim Goff, owners. Nine charming rooms with private baths, six with fireplaces. One handicapped accessible unit has fireplace. Rates: $85 to $105. Includes full breakfast and wine and cheese on Saturdays. Honeymoon cottage with Roman tub and fireplace, $135. No smoking; no pets; two very friendly outdoor cats live on the property; MasterCard/Visa. ISOMATA (Idyllwild School of Music and Art) concerts in summer, fishing, hiking, cross-country skiing nearby.

DIRECTIONS: will be provided on request.

Left, splendid craftsmanship and, above, elaborate details make this house a gem.

MOREY MANSION

A magnificent accomplishment

Master shipbuilder and craftsman David Morey built this mansion as testimony of love to his wife Sarah. The exterior of the house, built in 1889, is extraordinary in its combination of styles. The Russian Orthodox onion dome, French mansard roof of the two-story tower, the English fan over the front stairway, the Italian balustrades, and the Chinese-style veranda, all painted in various tones of browns and beiges accented with green, combine to make Morey Mansion breathtaking. Even the windows change from one story to the next, from traditional to arched to gothic. In the daylight the structure is massive; at dusk it glows with sensitive lighting; at night it glistens like a fairy-tale castle.

Fortunately, the elegance of the home remains unspoiled inside and out. Leaded beveled glass windows imported from Belgium in the front bay windows of the parlor and dining room are beautifully preserved. The original burgundy velvet

Parisian portiers trimmed with tapestry still hang in the parlor. All the parlor furniture is carved with Grecian women to match Morey's carvings on the fireplace. In the circular bay there is a grand player piano, with each key able to sound twenty volumes, and a working original Edison record player.

Much of the house tells the story of Morey's wife Sarah, who sold thousands of orange seedlings to raise the twenty thousand dollars that made this dream house possible. Carvings of orange blossoms are everywhere, in the wood and on every piece of hardware in the house, from the doorknobs to the drawer pulls.

To stay in this mansion is to experience first hand the life of one who was prosperous, imaginative, highly skilled, and deeply in love.

MOREY MANSION, 190 Terracina Boulevard, Redlands, CA 92373; (909) 793-7970; Dolly Tavares Wimer, manager. Five guest rooms, including one suite, with private and shared baths. Rates: $109 to $185. Includes a generous continental breakfast in formal dining room. No smoking; no children under 14; no pets; all credit cards.

DIRECTIONS: midway between Los Angeles and Palm Springs on I-10, six miles east of San Bernardino. Take Alabama exit south, follow "H" (hospital) signs, 2.6 miles to Terracina and Olive Ave.

The Heather Suite.

BRACKEN FERN MANOR

A Bugsy Segal hangout

The neat-as-a-pin interior of this 1920s Tudor-style inn looks so new that you would never guess it was once owned by Bugsy Segal and run by mobsters as a clubhouse for gambling and prostitution. A secret tunnel (still in evidence via a trap door in the living room floor) led from Bracken Fern across the street to the Tudor Hose, where the gambling took place. In those days Lake Arrowhead was a perfect spot for a clubhouse—whenever there was a hint of a raid on its way up the mountain, the slot machines disappeared into the wall and roulette wheels dropped into the floor.

Situated only five minutes from Lake Arrowhead, Bracken Fern Manor is one of the nicest B&B's in

Left, the diaphonous Bridal Suite.

the San Bernardino Mountains. On the main level is a tastefully furnished living room, game room, and library. Upstairs, each of the immaculate guest rooms are decorated in a fresh country style with brass, iron, and wicker beds. In the third-floor attic, where the ceilings are dramatically pitched, are three suites. The one departure from the country theme is the elegant Bridal Suite which is swathed in soft, newlywed white from floor to skylit ceiling. White gauze encloses the four-poster canopy bed and a white bridal veil hangs on the standing mirror. A basket of bath toys—rubber duckies, squirt guns, and sailboats—sit at the whirlpool tub for two, inviting a bit of play.

BRACKEN FERN MANOR, 815 Arrowhead Villas Rd., PO Box 1006, Lake Arrowhead, CA 92352; (909) 337-8557; Fax (909) 337-3323; Cheryl Weaver, owner. Open all year. Ten rooms, including Bridal Suite, all with private baths. Rates: $75 to $175, including full breakfast. Children welcome; smoking allowed outside only; Spanish spoken; no pets; all credit cards accepted. Hiking, fishing, horseback riding, and lake swimming nearby. Summer wine tastings offered at the inn. Mulberry Tree, Royal Oak, and Woody's Boat House recommended for dining.

DIRECTIONS: from Hwy. 18 east, turn left on Arrowhead Villas Rd.

The living room.

Uncle Will's Room.

THE KNICKERBOCKER MANSION

A 1940s mountain lodge

The Knickerbocker Mansion has the nostalgic feel of a 1940s mountain lodge. Handcrafted entirely from logs, the three-story mansion sits prominently on an evergreen and grass-covered hill above Big Bear Lake. Its rustic wood interior, big stone fireplace, and old rockers on the covered porches are exactly as they were 70 years ago. The sound of Big Band music playing completes the picture.

The living room is comfortably cluttered with velvet sofas and memorabilia such as an old Victrola and pipe collection. The double-sided fireplace faces both the living room and a sunny breakfast room. A massive split-log staircase leads upstairs to several homespun, country-style guest rooms with shared baths. Calico is a favorite because of its access to the porch. Uncle Will's Room (named after the owner's distant cousin, Will Rogers) sports a rustic Old West theme, complete with saddle, spurs, and Indian relics. On the third floor, where the attic once was, is a Penthouse Suite. It is so wide that additional twin bed nooks flank either side of the main bed. Four more contemporary rooms and a suite are in a separate carriage house up the hill.

Guests awaken to the comforting aroma of coffee and mouth-watering smells of breakfast sizzling away in the kitchen. After the hearty meal some guests set out on a hiking trail which starts out right from the lodge. Less adventurous souls might be content to sink into the hot tub or a hammock under the pines.

THE KNICKERBOCKER MANSION, 869 S. Knickerbocker Rd., PO Box 3661, Big Bear Lake, CA 92315; (800) 785-5535; (909) 866-8221; Fax (909) 866-6942; Clee Langley & Karen Bowers, owners. Open all year. Nine rooms and two suites; all with private baths except for two rooms with one shared bath. Rates: $75 to $225, including full breakfast. Children welcome; no smoking; no pets; Japanese, German, and Spanish spoken; all credit cards accepted. Hiking, mountain biking, lake activities, and skiing (snow & water) nearby. Weddings and specialty weekends can be arranged. Madlon's, The Iron Squirrel, and Log Cabin recommended for dining.

DIRECTIONS: from Hwy. 18 in Big Bear Village, turn right at Knickerbocker Rd. and continue up the hill 1/2 mile.

LA MAIDA HOUSE

North Hollywood Mediterranean villa

Italian artisans, brought here in the 1920s, adorned this seven-thousand-square-foot Sicilian mansion with ironwork, woodwork, marble, and fountains. Built on a grand scale, it is a villa not unlike those found on the Mediterranean.

The splendor of magnolia trees, blooming orchids, and three hundred varieties of roses can be viewed from the stained-glass-covered solarium, while the grace of a former era is reflected in the expansive living room and a dining room that seats thirty-four. There are several casual niches for relaxing, among them a multi-tiered couch in the game room and an upstairs porch for intimate dining.

The rooms, filled with fresh flowers from La Maida's gardens, are airy and elegant. An especially glorious one, in the main house, is the Cipresso Suite, with a white-canopied four-poster bed, wicker chaise, mirrored dressing room, and large blue-tiled bathroom. Downstairs the sun pours through white lace curtains, creating beautiful shadows at arched windows. Adding to the warmth are the stained-glass windows designed and made by Megan Timothy, La Maida's hostess.

The windows only hint at Megan's artistry, for in addition to working with clay, stone, and fabric, she is a highly skilled cook. A beautifully presented continental breakfast is an introduction to epicurean dinners that Megan can arrange and prepare for you and your guests.

LA MAIDA HOUSE & BUNGALOWS, 11159 La Maida Street, North Hollywood, CA 91601; (818) 769-3857, Fax (818) 753-9363; Megan Timothy, hostess. Four rooms in main house; seven in bungalows, all with private entrances, and several with Jacuzzi tubs and private gardens. Rates: $85 to $210. Includes generous continental breakfast. Phones and TVs in guest rooms. Answering machines provided on request. Business and social affairs arranged. No pets; no smoking; Visa/MasterCard/American Express. Chickens provide fresh eggs. Close to most major movie studios.

DIRECTIONS: please call ahead.

The Fontana Room, which has extra-long beds.

The Pier Suite.

VENICE BEACH HOUSE

Romantic lodgings near the beach

This restored house by the sea is a survivor of the splendid era of expansive two-story shingled beach houses and a more carefree way of life. Whether it is the breeze off the ocean, just steps away, or the easy hospitality of innkeeper Leslie Smith, one feels privileged to have discovered Venice Beach House.

Photographs of early Venice hang in the hallways, reminding guests of the days when this strip of Los Angeles marshland was turned into a simulation of Venice, Italy, complete with canals, bathhouses and boardwalks. Guest rooms are named after the eccentric characters who were instrumental in the resort's rise and subsequent decline.

The mood shifts from the contemporary elegance of the Pier Suite, a cool gray accented with rose, to Cora's Corner, a romantic pink and white wicker room. The room named after town father Abbott Kinney is covered in Scottish plaid wool, hunter green carpet, and dark wainscoting.

An additional pleasure is bathing side by side in a large, lush bathroom in claw-foot tubs, or enjoying the double Jacuzzi in James Peasgood's Room.

Breakfast on the veranda or in the sunny bay-window parlor usually includes cheeses, tomatoes, and meats as well as fruit, granola and a variety of breads.

You'll feel quite comfortable here. The inn is an informal, lovely place in which to relax near the sea.

VENICE BEACH HOUSE, No. 15, Thirtieth Avenue, Venice, CA 90291; (310) 823-1966, Fax (310) 823-1842; Vivian and Phil Boesch, owners; Leslie Smith, innkeeper. Nine rooms, five with private baths. Rates: $80 to $150, including full breakfast and afternoon refreshments. Children welcome; no pets; Visa/MasterCard/American Express. Smoking in porch areas. The Cheese & Olive Trattoria recommended for dining.

DIRECTIONS: from L.A. take 405 to Washington Street and make a right, heading towards the ocean. Turn right at Speedway and the house is on the right corner. Parking in the rear. Ten minutes from LAX.

THE INN AT 657

Five elegant suites

The Inn at 657, the closest bed and breakfast to downtown Los Angeles, was built in the 1930's as an apartment house. Innkeeper Patsy Humiston Carter, a retired trial lawyer, restored the building in 1991 and created five elegant suites complete with goosedown comforters, ironed sheets, bouquets of fresh roses and gladiolus, and refrigerators stocked with homemade goodies.

The suites vary in size and mood. The Oriental Blue Suite, for example, is attractively light, boasting a large living room in teals and corals, with silk furnishings and a Turkish rug. A ceremonial kimono hangs on the wall. The fully equipped kitchen is fresh and spotless.

Down a flowery walkway, in an apartment to the rear, is the dining room, where the table is laid with sterling silver and cut crystal for breakfast. Patsy's love of cooking is one of the reasons she turned to innkeeping. She buys her fruit directly from the downtown produce market and whips up such delights as Italian frittatas with ham, strawberry yogurt, and homemade bread pudding.

The Inn is situated in a neighborhood full of social contrast. Across the street is the elegant campus of Mount St. Mary's College, but also nearby are some pretty gritty areas. It's a fact of life in L.A. that you can't have one extreme without the other, and the Inn provides a safe harbor between the two.

THE INN AT 657, 657 West Twenty-Third Street, Los Angeles, CA 90007; (213) 741-2200, (800) 347-7512. Patsy Humiston Carter, proprietor. Open all year. Rates: $95 single occupancy, double $15 extra, including full breakfast. Jacuzzi on the premises. No pets; no smoking; Spanish spoken; no credit cards. Close to USC, Los Angeles Convention Center, financial district, Shrine Auditorium, Civic Center, Music Center. Engine Company No. 28, El Jarrito for dining.

DIRECTIONS: from I-110 south, exit at Adams and turn right on 23rd Street. The Inn is one block west of Figueroa.

LORD MAYOR'S INN B&B

Sensitively restored

This pristine blue and white Edwardian house, once the home of the first mayor of Long Beach, was meticulously renovated by Laura and Reuben Brasser.

Throughout the warm wood interior is a mix of family heirlooms and antiques, including fine armoires, rockers and distinctive beds. In Margarita's Room are two eighteenth-century Austrian beds, while the Hawaiian Room features an elaborately carved Hawaiian wedding bed complete with pineapple and hula girl motifs. The many rag rugs over the wood floors were crafted by Laura, as were the window coverings and dried flower arrangements.

The hearty breakfasts range from scrambled eggs and popovers to buttermilk pancakes. Laura makes her coffee cakes, jams and lemon curd from scratch.

All the highlights of downtown Long Beach—the Queen Mary, convention center, World Trade Center and Terrace Theatre—are only minutes away from this historic landmark.

LORD MAYOR'S INN BED & BREAKFAST, 435 Cedar Avenue, Long Beach, CA 90802; (310) 436-0324. Laura and Reuben Brasser, innkeepers. Open all year. Five rooms, all with private baths. Rates: $85 to $105, including a full breakfast and evening refreshments. One-night mystery packages available. Children accepted; no pets; smoking allowed on deck only; Freisian, Dutch, and Danish spoken; Visa/MasterCard/American Express/Discover. Many restaurants nearby.

DIRECTIONS: from I-710 south, exit at 6th St. After three blocks, turn right on Cedar Ave. Inn is on the right.

The Americana Attic Suite on the third floor.

SALISBURY HOUSE B&B

Classic Craftsman

This 1909 California Craftsman house, the first bed and breakfast in Los Angeles, is centrally located in the historic West Adams district near downtown—a once-affluent neighborhood which fell into decline after the Santa Monica Freeway cut through it. Although visitors may be put off by the surrounding area, all is forgotten when you turn onto spacious 20th Street and enter the oasis of the Salisbury House.

Used as a location for several movie productions, the Salisbury House is a refreshing sight. Classic Craftsman-style wood beams outline the immaculately restored home, while jacarandas, roses, and bougainvillea bloom at the entry. The large living room and dining room feature an abundance of wood paneling, wood-beamed ceilings, original leaded glass and whimsical light fixtures.

The dining room table is nicely set for breakfast

Left. The front entrance, blooming with jacarandas, roses, and bougainvillea.

with a lace tablecloth, white linens, and pink Depression glass. Breakfast specialties include strawberry waffles, spicy Mexican casseroles with cornbread, and country casseroles with potatoes and fresh herbs from the herb garden in back.

The second-floor guest rooms are fresh and floral, with old-fashioned furnishings and lots of nice decorative touches.

SALISBURY HOUSE BED & BREAKFAST, 2273 W. 20th Street, Los Angeles, CA 90018; (213) 737-7817, (800) 373-1778, Fax (213) 737-7817; Sue and Jay German, innkeepers. Open all year. Five rooms and suites, two with shared bath. Rates: $70 to $95, single; $75 to $100, double, including full breakfast. Children accepted; no pets; no smoking; some Spanish and French spoken; Visa/MasterCard/American Express/Discover. Inn is 10 to 20 minutes from every major sight in Los Angeles. A restaurant guide, written by the innkeeper, is available.

DIRECTIONS: one block north of I-10 between Western and Arlington Streets.

Innkeeper Sue German.

CHANNEL ROAD INN

No expense was spared on the décor

When you step into the serene, lightly-scented living room, it is hard to believe that hectic Los Angeles is just around the corner and that the inn is set one block from the ocean. The innkeepers have an effective antidote for unwinding from city affairs— grab some milk and cookies, then head straight to the beach on one of their bicycles.

The 1910 building, a rare West Coast example of shingle-clad Colonial Revival architecture, was originally built in another neighborhood of Santa Monica for Thomas McCall, a Scottish oil and cattle baron. After being moved to its present location, the house stood abandoned and defaced with graffiti for twelve years until it was lovingly restored by builder Susan Zolla and friends in 1988. From the goose-down pillows and thousand-dollar mattresses to the appliquéd lace bed coverings, no expense has been spared on décor.

Elegant country is the theme throughout this inn.

The exquisite living room features pastel silk furnishings atop a lavender Chinese rug, vases of fresh roses, a Batchelder-tiled fireplace, and a piano covered with framed photos of the McCall family.

The fourteen guest rooms, many with hardwood floors, were inspired by a variety of interior designers. Room Eleven appeals to romantics, with its gauze-canopied antique pine bed. Creamy-colored Room Twelve is tucked away in a quiet corner with an ocean view. Room Seven, in sophisticated gray and black, is a favorite with businessmen. Honeymooners love the fireplace suite and canopy bed in Room Six.

Guests are pampered with terry robes, spacious private bathrooms, and bubble bath; and wine and cheese are served afternoons in a sunny library. An outdoor spa rests against the flowery hillside. Breakfast includes such specialties as chocolate chip coffee cake, homemade müesli, or bread pudding with boysenberries.

CHANNEL ROAD INN, 219 West Channel Road, Santa Monica, CA 90402; (310) 459-1920; Susan Zolla, owner, Kathy Jensen, manager. Open all year. Fourteen rooms with private baths. Rates: $85 to $225 per room, including full breakfast and afternoon refreshments. Children welcome; no pets; smoking outside only; Spanish and French spoken; Visa/MasterCard/American Express. Handicapped accessible.

DIRECTIONS: Freeway 10 west to Pacific Coast Highway (Rte. 1). Go north for 2 miles to West Channel Road.

CENTRAL COAST

LA MER

European hospitality and apple strudel

Entering La Mer is like stepping into a scene from *Heidi Comes to America*, if there were such a book. Gisela (pronounced GHEE-zel-la) Baida often dons a peasant dress or a dirndl to greet her guests; her blond curls, infectious smile, and light German accent complete the picture of a Bavarian maiden.

Gisela and her husband Mike run this five-room hostelry with old-world hospitality. Guests wake up to a buffet of müesli, Black Forest ham, cheeses, apple strudel, torte, fruits, and if they're lucky, *traenchenkuchen*, a German cheesecake with a meringue top. Fresh-squeezed orange juice and brewed regular or decaffeinated mocha-java coffee complement the elaborate spread.

Continuing the European theme, each room represents a country. The Captain's Coje ("hideaway"), a Norwegian room, features a ship's bed with high sides, a hanging net with starfish and cork floats, even books of Norse mythology and sailing stories. In contrast, the French Madame Pompadour Room sets an elegant style with a gracefully curved walnut bed from France that is complemented by the Renaissance prints and tapestry on the walls.

The atmosphere, though, is decidedly California casual. Gisela offers a special mid-week package that includes therapeutic massages, hot mineral baths, and a carriage ride to a nearby winery. Cookies and candies are left out for nighttime nibblers, and all guests receive a small bottle of wine or sparkling cider as an extension of the hosts' generosity.

LA MER EUROPEAN BED AND BREAKFAST, 411 Poli Street, Ventura, CA 93001; (805) 643-3600, Fax (805) 653-7329; Gisela and Mike Baida, owners. Five rooms with private baths, one has wood-burning stove, all but one have private entrance. Rates: $80 to $155, includes ample Bavarian buffet breakfast. Children 13 years old and up welcome; no smoking indoors; no pets (Yorkshire terrier, Mommy the cat, and rabbits are in residence); German and Spanish spoken; Visa/MasterCard/American Express. Golf, tennis, boat rental nearby. Midweek packages available. Five hens provide fresh eggs.

DIRECTIONS: from Los Angeles, take US-101 north to the California St. Exit, make a right, and come up three blocks. California St. dead ends at Poli; make a left onto Poli St. After 200 feet, you'll see the B&B on the right. Outdoor parking is available in the rear.

The Madame Pompador Room.

The Violet Room.

The Chinois Room.

THE FERN OAKS INN

Spanish Revival with 1930s ambience

The Fern Oaks Inn is situated in a lovely neighborhood of Santa Paula, a quiet, agricultural town in the heart of Ventura County. Built in 1929, this peach-colored Spanish Revival home is encircled by mature oaks, citrus and fruit trees, and over seventy varieties of roses.

Inside, all the 30's details—built-in cabinets, glass doorknobs, and original tilework—have been restored to a warm glow by innkeeper and interior designer Cheryl Conroy. The living room is highlighted by a Batchelder-designed fireplace, an Erté bronze, and china that Cheryl has hand painted. In the formal dining room is an exquisite collection of antique cruets and pickle castors.

Upstairs, the Violet and Chinois Rooms are de-

Left, the inn and its dining room.

lightfully crisp and fresh, with original porcelain tubs in their private bathrooms. The Williamsburg Room features a four-poster pineapple bed and traditional American décor. Casablanca, the most requested room, is more tropical, with a private sun porch that overlooks the inn's swimming pool and the Topa Topa Mountains.

Breakfast is a full, sit-down affair, usually served in a small solarium lined by Palladian windows. On Sunday mornings guests are treated to New Orleans caramelized French toast topped with sour cream, sliced strawberries, and a variety of other fresh fruits. Other house specialties include eggs Oscar served with homemade buttermilk biscuits, and dried cherry and cranberry scones.

THE FERN OAKS INN, 1025 Ojai Rd., Santa Paula, CA 93060; (805) 525-7747; Jim and Cheryl Conroy, owners. Open all year. Four rooms, all with private baths and air conditioning. Rates: $95 to $110 weekends; $10 less weekdays; including full gourmet breakfast. Children welcome; smoking permitted outside only; no pets; no credit cards. Outdoor heated swimming pool on premises. Santa Paula Theater Center, Santa Paula Airport (known as the "Antique Airplane Capital of the World"), Wheeler Hot Springs, and Ojai nearby. Glen Tavern, Logsdons, and L'Auberge recommended for dining.

DIRECTIONS: from SR-126, exit at 10th St., proceed 1 mi. north to Ojai Rd. and bear right.

Wooden sculpture by Boyd Wright.

OJAI MANOR HOTEL

An artistic approach

Innkeeper Mary Nelson's stylish good taste and the exciting sculpture created by her partner, Boyd Wright, harmonize perfectly at the Ojai Manor. The place is immediately engaging because of the very personal combination of fine, traditional, turn-of-the-century furnishings with modern prints, collages, and paintings by friends and associates.

Built in 1874, the manor is reported to be the oldest building in Ojai and served the "heart and soul" of the community as a schoolhouse, town hall, and hotel before it was bought in the 1950s by Mary's family. Just one block from the town's main street and a few blocks from a wonderful outdoor used bookstore and several highly recommended restaurants, the manor attracts low-keyed travelers who come here to relax and do little else, which is not to imply that the more active will find little to do. Mary recommends a trip up to Wheeler's Hot Springs for the massages and mineral baths, or a walk over to Libby Park during the jazz and classical music festivals.

In the evening, guests can sink into deep blue-velvet couches next to the fireplace and have a glass of sherry. Or they can pull up a big willow chair near the pot-bellied stove in the dining room. Whatever they do, they will be surrounded by the great variety of original artworks that make the manor special.

OJAI MANOR HOTEL, 210 East Matilija, Ojai, CA 93023; (805) 646-0961; Mary Nelson, host. Six tastefully appointed rooms that share three baths. Rates $90 to $100. Includes buffet continental breakfast of fresh fruits and fresh baking, such as cinnamon rolls or apple strudel. Children over 12; no smoking; pets negotiable. A bit of Spanish spoken. Visa/MasterCard. One block from Ojai Avenue.

DIRECTIONS: from US-101 take Rte. 33 for 14 miles to Ojai exit. After the first stoplight in Ojai go one mile to fourth light and turn left onto Signal Street. One block to Matilija Street and turn right.

Mission bed from a small Western hotel.

An elaborately decorated guest room.

INN ON SUMMER HILL

Elaborate "country French" décor

The Inn on Summer Hill is a fresh new bed and breakfast built in the Arts and Crafts style, but the sixteen guest rooms could best be described as elaborate Country French. All the beds are canopied imaginatively with yards and yards of imported fabrics. Contrasting patterns are mixed together in each room (a checked canopy, floral quilt, and striped dust ruffle, for instance), creating a riot of color that looks amazingly delightful.

Mabel Shults, the owner and designer, obviously had a field day with the pattern-suffused interior decorating. Even the paintings, done by local Santa Barbara artists, were commissioned specifically to fit in with the décor of each room.

Many of the bedrooms have pine beds, hardwood floors, beamed ceilings, and switch-on fireplaces. Pine armoires conceal a television, VCR, stereo cassette player, (with speakers in both the bathroom and bedroom), terry robes, ironing board, and refrigerator stocked with mineral water. The bathrooms are outfitted with hair dryers, Caswell-Massey soaps, and Jacuzzi jets in the tubs. Hot water pots with coffee and tea fixings, along with your own morning newspaper, all add up to an impressive list of amenities.

Varying each day, a full breakfast of either waffles, quiche, blintzes, eggs Florentine, or crêpes is served in the country-style breakfast room; then there is an afternoon repast of wine, cheese, crackers, and cookies. Beds are turned down with Sees chocolates on the goose-down comforters. After dining out, guests may return to the inn for a dessert of either bread pudding, white chocolate mousse pie or fruit tarts, and coffee.

The Inn on Summer Hill has an outdoor spa surrounded by white latticework, as well as whimsical bird houses perched here and there. Sandy Summerland Beach is only six blocks away, on the other side of busy Highway 101.

INN ON SUMMER HILL, 2520 Lillie Ave., Summerland, CA 93067; (800) 845-5566, (805) 969-9998, Fax (805) 565-9946; Paul and Mabel Shults, owners. Open all year. Sixteen rooms with canopied king, queen, double queen beds and Jacuzzis, fireplaces, and ocean views; 2-room suite with 2 fireplaces and wet bar. Rates: $160 to $295 per room, including full breakfast, afternoon wine, cheese, fruit, and late evening dessert and coffee. Not appropriate for children; no pets; no smoking indoors; all credit cards accepted. Large choice of excellent restaurants in nearby Santa Barbara and Montecito.

DIRECTIONS: from US-101 take Evans exit and go south on Lillie to inn on left.

The Sun Room's private deck overlooks the gardens.

SIMPSON HOUSE INN

Immaculate and elegant grandeur

Although situated on just under an acre of land, the elegant and immaculate Simpson House Inn conveys all the grandeur of a larger estate. Formal eugenia hedges at sidewalk's edge screen the house from the quiet tree-lined street. On the other side, magnolias, mature oaks, and pittisporums punctuate the manicured lawn and flowered borders add a burst of color to the tranquil scene.

When Glyn and Linda Davies bought the property in 1976, the trees were bare and the lawn was a brown patch. The house was in equally bad condition. With love and care, the Davies made the house a gracious home. Their children grown, they decided to turn the 1874 Italianate Victorian into a bed and breakfast. To do so, they fought the city with a fierce determination and won the right to accept guests.

The Davies' attitude toward their house is uncompromising. All of the antique-filled rooms and the many common areas are spacious and spotless. Cotton sheets and European goose-down comforters dress the beds; the wraparound porch sports a teak floor; and breakfast items—scones, popovers, or muffins—are made with as little refined sugar as possible.

Resident innkeeper Gillean Wilson attends to the details that give guests an extraordinary feeling of being pampered. She reminds people of the complimentary bicycles, sets out a truly appetizing array of hors d'oeuvres in the afternoon, and invites visitors to see the chickens and ducks at the back of the property.

An overnight barely does the house justice. Staying at the Simpson House Inn is an exercise in self-indulgence.

SIMPSON HOUSE INN, 121 East Arrellaga Street, Santa Barbara, CA 93101; (805) 963-7067; Glyn and Linda Davies, owners; Gillean Wilson, resident innkeeper. Fourteen elegant rooms, all with private baths. Rates: $110 to $250. Includes full gourmet breakfast and wine and hors d'oeuvres in the afternoon. Children welcome; smoking on the rear veranda only; no pets; Spanish spoken; major credit cards. Complimentary bicycles and croquet available. Full agenda of sporting activities, antiques shops, and trolley tour in and around town. Located on one acre of English gardens.

DIRECTIONS: from US-101 north, take Santa Barbara St. exit and turn right; go 1½ miles to East Arrellaga. Inn is in first block. From Hwy. 101 south, take Mission St. exit; turn left and go 7 blocks to Anacapa St. and turn right, then turn left onto Arrellaga St.

THE TIFFANY INN

Exquisite antiques

Within walking distance of shops, restaurants, and theaters, and only half a mile to the beach, The Tiffany Inn is situated in the heart of downtown Santa Barbara.

The MacDonalds have placed extraordinarily fine pieces throughout the house. Antiques range from formal, such as the elaborately carved Victorian Renaissance bed and armoire in the Somerset Room, to the casual country oak of the Rose Garden Room. The velvet puff-sleeved drapery, the white lace curtains, and the beautifully upholstered chairs reflect the meticulous care and straightforward elegance that typifies this inn. The restoration of this stately mansion was clearly a labor of love for Carol and Larry.

THE TIFFANY INN, 1323 De La Vina, Santa Barbara, CA 93101; (805) 963-2283; Carol & Larry MacDonald, hosts. Seven rooms, all with private baths and fireplaces. Rates: $115 to $200. Includes full breakfast of quiche, crêpes, French toast or eggs, and evening wine and hors d'oeuvres. Children over 12; smoking on patio; off-street parking, Visa/MasterCard/ American Express. Inquire about mid-season and corporate rates.

DIRECTIONS: from the south on US-101, exit at State Street and go right (north) onto State. Proceed 9 blocks and turn left onto Sola. Go 2 blocks and turn left onto De La Vina. From the north on US-101, exit at Mission Street and turn left (east) onto Mission. Proceed for 3 blocks and make a right onto De La Vina.

The Somerset Room has this handsome Renaissance bed.

THE CHESHIRE CAT

Alice in Ashleyland

Lewis Carroll would be delighted with the wonderland created at The Cheshire Cat, two beige and white Victorian houses in the heart of residential Santa Barbara. Meticulously landscaped grounds are enhanced by a high-peaked, white lattice gazebo. White porch railings and columns, white lace curtains in the windows, and white trim on the houses give The Cheshire Cat a polished look.

Each room is its own Lewis Carroll fantasy. Laura Ashley draperies, bedspreads, chair fabrics, and wallpapers are carefully coordinated in color and pattern. Even the lamp shades are covered in fabric; sapphire and white in The Mock Turtle chamber, plum and cream in The Mad Hatter. The rooms have a precious but romantic flair. The carpeting is plush, the satin comforters alluring.

Breakfast is served in the comfortable Country dining room or on the brick patio, and fine English china patterned with small strawberries adds a touch of elegance to the continental fare. Bailey's Bristol Cream awaits guests upon arrival, as does a box of chocolates from Santa Barbara's famous Chocolate Gallery. The large white "all-seeing cat" adds to the fantasy.

THE CHESHIRE CAT, 36 West Valerio Street, Santa Barbara, CA 93101, (805) 569-1610; Chris Dunstan, owner; Jennifer Martin, manager. Fourteen rooms in two adjacent houses and carriage house, all with private baths; four with Jacuzzis in the room, three with fireplaces, and several with patios. Rates: $125 to $249; special midweek rates. Includes full breakfast served on outdoor patio or in dining room and wine and cheese in evenings. No small children; no smoking; no pets; Visa/MasterCard.

DIRECTIONS: from the south on US-101 at Arellaga exit, take a right. Proceed on Arellaga and make a left onto Chapala. Go 1 block to Valerio; the inn is on the corner. From the north on US-101 take the Mission Street exit. Take a right on De La Vina, a left on Valerio, and proceed 2 blocks.

Alice's Room

The Honeymoon Suite.

THE PARSONAGE

Room with a view

This Queen Anne Victorian was the parsonage for the Episcopalian church over one hundred years ago. Perched on the rising foothills leading up to the Santa Barbara Mission, it is the only bed and breakfast here with ocean views.

In the living room, an emerald green and Burgundy Oriental carpet serves as a vibrant backdrop for the antiques and original redwood woodwork that are stylishly combined with modern furnishings.

Upstairs, the Las Flores room, with its unusual marble-topped sideboard and antique armoire, recaptures the era when this building was a rectory. The Peacock Room, with its stained-glass window, is awash in blues and whites and carpeted in mauve. The Honeymoon suite, with Jacuzzi and expansive views of the ocean, has perhaps the best view in the city of downtown Santa Barbara.

Ed and Lee Lewis, the charming resident innkeepers, serve up a gourmet breakfast that delights guests every time: eggs Benedict, or strawberry oven-baked French toast; Dutch babies (a baked fruit-filled pancake), and a variety of fruit breads baked on the premises.

The spacious outdoor deck is made for sun worshippers, and it is tempting to curl up in one of the lounge chairs with a good book. Breakfast is often served at one of the umbrella-covered tables. If light exercise is in order, the famous mission is a short, pleasant walk away.

THE PARSONAGE, 1600 Olive Street, Santa Barbara, CA 93101, (805) 962-9336, (800) 775-0352; Ed and Lee Lewis, innkeepers. Open all year. Six rooms, including one suite, all with private baths, 2 with fireplaces, 2 with Jacuzzis, 2 with ocean views; 3 additional suites in nearby house suitable for families. Rates: $95 to $185, including full gourmet breakfast. Children welcome; no pets; smoking outside only; Visa/MasterCard/American Express.

DIRECTIONS: from south on US-101 exit onto State Street. From State take a right at Arrellaga Street and proceed to Olive St. From north on US-101 exit onto Mission Street. Go to end of Mission and make a right onto Laguna for 1 block and left onto Olive.

Left, four shades of rose grace the restored building. A multitude of windows illuminate the rooms, as in the one above.

CRYSTAL ROSE INN

A spectacularly romantic mecca

This 1885 landmark home, once surrounded by walnut tree farms, continues to dominate the horizon of the farmlands of San Luis Obispo County. Painted in four shades of rose, it rises toward the sky, a majestic fifty-five-foot four-story Victorian.

The inn has become a romantic mecca. More than four hundred brides have walked along the thirty-foot rose arbor to the gazebo to meet their grooms. Celebrating anniversaries at the Crystal Rose Inn is a tradition many couples still honor.

The romance doesn't end there. Champagne can be ordered for breakfast, which may feature wild rose pancakes with apple sauce and country bacon, a vegetable-sausage frittata, or a strawberry Belgian waffle with ham roll. High tea with crystal and candlelight, tea sandwiches, and chocolate-dipped fruit are served in the lovely Tearoom, and wine and hors d'oeuvres are offered in the evening.

Finally, the beautiful grounds have extensive Victorian gardens planted with roses, Icelandic poppies, daisies, a gazebo, and a sculptural water fountain. There is croquet to try your hand at as well as a bicycle built for two.

For guests who like to pass a quiet evening, there is a large parlor perfect for deliberating over a chess board or indulging in a lively conversation. The nearby Great American Melodrama and Vaudeville Show is recommended for those who like to hiss and boo at the villain.

CRYSTAL ROSE INN. 789 Valley Road, Arroyo Grande, CA 93420; (805) 481-1854; Bonnie Royster and Dona Nolan, owners. Eleven rooms, seven with private bath; remaining four rooms share two baths. Each room decorated in keeping with Victorian period. Rates: $85 to $175 with full breakfast. Children over sixteen; no pets; smoking in the restaurant and gardens, but not in the house. Two entertaining cats and Rose, the collie dog in residence.

DIRECTIONS: located 200 miles north of L.A. and 250 miles south of San Francisco. Take Traffic Way exit from US-101 North. Turn left at the stop sign onto Fair Oaks. From 101 South take Fair Oaks exit and turn right on Fair Oaks. From Fair Oaks turn left onto Valley Road for ¼ mi. to inn.

The formal parlor.

The Olallieberry Room.

The San Simeon Room.

THE OLALLIEBERRY INN

In the quaint town of Cambria

Dotted with a mix of English half-timbered, log and Victorian buildings, the quaint town of Cambria is divided into two sections—the west side near the beach, and the east side, which is wooded with pines. Just a short stroll from the east side of downtown is The Olallieberry Inn, one of the oldest buildings in town.

Built in 1873, the rather plain, Greek Revival façade is brightened by an herb garden (featured recently in *Sunset*) that is lovingly tended by innkeepers Peter and Carol Ann Irsfeld. Just off the herb garden is another "secret garden," and behind the inn, overlooking Santa Rosa Creek, is their "butterfly garden."

Left, the garden and the clapboard inn.

Not only does Peter love to garden, but he does the cooking as well. In addition to wines from local vineyards and fresh garden vegetables with a dip, his afternoon hors d'oeuvres might include baked brie in puff pastry, goat cheese with homebaked foccacia, or pizza with black olives, roasted garlic, and fresh rosemary. On the morning menu are freshly baked muffins, granola, yogurt, fruit, and a hot entrée such as stuffed French toast, or eggs baked in a hash brown potato crust, or fresh fruit crêpes. This is served in an informal, wicker and sun-filled gathering room with French doors opening to the back deck and lawn.

The guest quarters, several with gas fireplaces, are furnished in soft colors and antique beds. Three rooms, including one suite, have been added to the newly remodeled Carriage House next door.

THE OLALLIEBERRY INN, 2476 Main St., Cambria, CA 93428; (805) 927-3222; Fax (805) 927-0202; Peter & Carol Ann Irsfeld, owners. Open all year. Eight rooms and one suite, all with private baths (three detached). Rates: $85 to $175, including full gourmet breakfast and afternoon wine and hors d'oeuvres. Childen not encouraged; smoking allowed outdoors only; no pets; Visa/MasterCard. Hearst Castle, Moonstone Beach, antiquing and art galleries nearby.
DIRECTIONS: from Hwy. 1, exit at Main St. and proceed toward downtown Cambria.

The exterior of the log house.

The Galway Room.

J. PATRICK HOUSE

Warm and cozy throughout

The J. Patrick House blends well with its misty, wooded setting above Cambria. Built of logs, the main house overlooks a forest of tall Monterey pines. You would almost think you were in the mountains, yet the ocean is only minutes away.

In the main house is a living room and sunny breakfast room overlooking a garden of delicate flowers. Upstairs, the mini-suite Clare is the most requested room. The other seven guest rooms, each named after Irish counties, are in a separate cedar Carriage House with its own parlor.

The country décor is warm and cozy throughout, enhanced by pretty patchwork quilts, bent willow furnishings, dried flower wreaths, and stuffed animals, many of which are for sale. Every room has a wood-burning fireplace to ward off the chilly nights.

In the early evening innkeepers Mel and Barbara Schwimmer mingle with their guests before the living room fire over a selection of French and local wines, crackers, and various homemade dips such as smoked salmon spread, spicy ginger eggplant dip,

Left, innkeepers Barbara and Mel Schwimmer.

J. PATRICK HOUSE, 2990 Burton Dr., Cambria, CA 93428; (800) 341-5258; (805) 927-3812; Barbara & Mel Schwimmer, owners. Open all year. Eight rooms, including one mini-suite, all with private baths and wood-burning fireplaces. Rates: $110-150, including continental plus breakfast, afternoon wine and hors d'oeuvres. Children welcome in Clare Room; no smoking; no pets; all credit cards accepted. Hearst Castle, tide pools, wineries, restaurants, and shopping nearby. Ian's, Robin's, and Sow's Ear recommended for dining.

DIRECTIONS: from Hwy. 1, exit at Burton Dr. and proceed east for 1/4 mile.

and vegetarian pâté. Before leaving the inn at night (they live just down the road), the Schwimmers place milk and homebaked cookies in very room.

Each morning guests are served fresh fruit with a choice of toppings—yogurt, delicious house granola, and fresh local raisins. Irish soda bread and muffins follow, again with a selection of homemade spreads. It's the time the Schwimmers spend with their guests and all of these homemade touches that make the J. Patrick House such a personal inn.

The rustic Clare Room.

The Vineyard Suite.

THE BALLARD INN

Celebrates the past with deft touches

The tone of the inn is commemorative. Vintage photographs and memorabilia decorate each room of the inn and depict persons, events, or themes important to the heritage of the San Ynez Valley and the Santa Barbara wine country.

Researched and decorated by co-owner Nan Allison-Stone, each room is unique. In the room honoring early settler and trapper Davy Brown, a fireplace built with stones from the San Ynez River, a distressed oak floor, and log-paneled walls simulate the interior of an authentic log cabin. In contrast, the Wildflower Room, which highlights native flowers, is as sweet and lovely as its name implies. Decorated in lavender, pink, and coral, it has a floral duvet-covered quilt and gentle sewing rocker. The Equestrian Room is outfitted to celebrate a rich history of

horse breeding in the valley. The Jaradao Room plays tribute to the native Chumash Indians and the Vineyard Suite has bent willow furniture, champagne colored walls, and a grape-motif duvet.

The inn and its cuisine may be described in one word—expansive. Guests may "design" their own multiple course breakfast from a buffet of fruits, cheeses, breads, and a choice of splendid entrées. There are several common rooms, including a den with a VCR and a large living room where one may enjoy hors d'oeuvres and local wine. Café Chardonnay, an onsite restaurant, offers creative wine country cuisine.

The San Ynez Valley is a special place. Twelve wineries are within close proximity of the inn. Large ranches and several world-class Arabian horse breeders are also nearby.

THE BALLARD INN, 2436 Baseline, Ballard, CA 93463; (805) 688-7770, Fax (805) 688-9560. Larry Stone and Steve Hyslop, owners; Kelly Robinson, innkeeper. Fifteen rooms, all with private baths, several with fireplaces. Rates: $160 to $195. Includes afternoon refreshments, cheeses, and hors d'oeuvres and incredible breakfast that just won't quit. Handicap access. Visa/MasterCard/American Express.

DIRECTIONS: from the north take US-101, to Rte. 154 to Los Olivos; turn south (right) on Alamo Pintado Road towards Ballard. From the south take US-101 to Rte. 246, through Solvang. Go north (left) on Alamo Pintado Road.

MONTEREY

THE JABBERWOCK

Enjoy a breakfast of Razzleberries

Named after the mythical character in Lewis Carroll's poem "Jabberwocky," this Jabberwock is a special bed and breakfast where two themes prevail. First, there is humor in everything that hosts Jim and Barbara Allen undertake. From the presentation of a tantalizing series of mysterious hors d'oeuvres at aperitif hour to the surprise breakfast, everything is a curiosity. Anything from Snarkleberry, Razzleberry, or Frabjous may appear on the menu. The guest rooms have names too: Tulgey Wood, Mome Rath, or Brillig.

The second prevailing theme at the Jabberwock is hospitality, a flair for which Barbara developed during thirteen years spent in the hotel industry. Everything is first quality here, from the lace-trimmed sheets to the special down comforters.

Details have been carefully attended to, such as writing first names of guests on a chalkboard, or leaving binoculars on windowsills for a bay view. Jim, a recently retired captain of the Los Angeles Fire Department, has his own style and penchant for fun, and it is well worth asking him for a tour in the British Beardmore taxi.

Once a convent, the Jabberwock makes a large, elegant home. The living room is luxurious, and the wraparound sun porch is especially inviting. Gardens and a waterfall only enhance what Jim and Barbara have created to make your visit to the Monterey Peninsula memorable.

THE JABBERWOCK. 598 Laine Street, Monterey, CA 93940; (408) 372-4777, Fax (408) 655-2946; Jim and Barbara Allen, hosts. Barbara speaks French, Danish, and Spanish. Seven rooms, three with private baths. Rates: $100 to $185. Includes imaginative, delicious breakfast, a delectable selection of hors d'oeuvres and warm cookies and milk before bed. No children; no pets; smoking outdoors; Visa/MasterCard. Popular English bull terrier in residence. Four blocks above Cannery Row and Monterey Bay aquarium.

DIRECTIONS: from Rte. 1 take Rte. 68 west for 2½ miles. Turn right onto Prescott and right onto Pine for one block and then turn left onto Hoffman. The Jabberwock is on the corner of Hoffman and Laine.

Special treats await guests at bed-time.

OLD MONTEREY INN

Casts a powerful, romantic spell

The Old Monterey Inn casts a powerful romantic spell over its guests. Conjuring up the days of grand country cottages, the half-timbered Tudor house stands regally in a quiet garden setting with secluded benches and a hammock at the end of paths that lead nowhere.

A huge live oak in back takes immediate center focus, adorned with pots of hanging fuchsias and geraniums as if they were Japanese lanterns. Tucked in by its base, a meditative stone bench calls attention to the brick walkway which eventually leads to the flower-adorned breakfast patio and formal rose garden, set off by Italian cypress trees, a flowering cherry, and the original owner's peonies.

Carmel Martin, Sr., the first elected mayor of Monterey, built this hospitable home in 1929, with an eye for elegance and enduring sophistication. Local craftsmen contributed to the details

Romance blooms within the picture-perfect Ashford Suite.

that make this inn so refreshingly different. Most notable is the dining room, a Mexican-influenced *sala* boasting hand-carved and painted ceiling panels, and an exquisite solid copper fireplace hood.

Current owners Ann and Gene Swett designed the spacious guest rooms to have a more modern, airy ambiance, enhanced by sitting areas, fireplaces, and plush goosedown comforters and pillows. Impeccably appointed, each room communicates restful luxury, whether amid chintz, lace, and ruffles or somber tones of umber and pale olive matched with natural rattan. The Ashford Suite and the private cottage are picture-perfect romantic studies, while the library, with its built-in floor-to-ceiling bookcases, sports its own unique appeal.

Complimentary soft drinks, a sherry and hors d'oeuvres hour, and afternoon cookies fill out the amenities here where casual graciousness reigns supreme.

The entrance welcomes you in.

OLD MONTEREY INN. 500 Martin Street, Monterey, CA 93940; (408) 375-8284, Fax (408) 375-6730; Gene and Ann Swett, owners. Closed Christmas. Ten charming rooms with private baths, most with fireplaces. Rates: $170 to $240. Includes full breakfast, afternoon cookies, and sherry and hors d'oeuvres in the evening. Not suitable for children; no smoking indoors; no pets; Visa/MasterCard. Aquarium, raceway, hot-air ballooning, shoreline recreation trail, and other sports and cultural activities nearby.

DIRECTIONS: take the Soledad/Moonras exit off Hwy. 1; proceed through the signal to Pacific St. and turn right onto Pacific. Go a mile and turn left onto Martin St.

RUSSELL ABRAHAM PHOTOGRAPH

THE COBBLESTONE INN

Where you get lots of attention

Stuffed animal fans will love the Cobblestone Inn. At least fifty bears dangle whimsically around the lobby alone, delighting both children and adults. Bears are literally everywhere—huddled in the living room, squeezed between the banisters, and most likely doing somersaults on your bed.

The bears, an original carousel horse, and hand-made crafts are a signature of the Post family, which owns two other inns on the Monterey Peninsula. There are many special touches offered at the Cobblestone Inn. Handwritten personalized welcome notes greet guests; balloons are presented for special occasions; complimentary soft drinks are found in a discreetly hidden refrigerator; beds are turned down with chocolates, a rose, and written proverb in the evening; your newspaper and freshly polished shoes can be delivered to your door in the morning.

And you will never go hungry with a full buffet breakfast, cookies and beverages available all day, and enough afternoon hors d'oeuvres (raw vegies, dip, French bread, paté and cheeses) to spoil your dinner.

The Cobblestone Inn was an ordinary two-storey Carmel motel until it underwent a total transformation in 1984. The central parking area was converted into a cobblestone courtyard of flowers and creepers, along with an outdoor patio with tables and chairs. The American country-style living-breakfast room has a large cobblestone fireplace and lots of literature on local activities. Guest rooms blend fresh country décor with modern comforts—television and phones included—and all have switch-button fireplaces made of (what else?)—cobblestones!

THE COBBLESTONE INN. Junipero Street near 8th P.O. Box 3185, Carmel, CA 93921; (408) 625-5222; Roger and Sally Post, owners; Ray Farnsworth, manager. Open all year. 24 rooms with private baths, fireplaces, and queen or king beds (only 2 rooms have tubs). Rates $95 to $175 double, including full breakfast of eggs, muffins, fruit, etc. Children welcome (2 and over $15 extra); no pets; smoking outside only; Vietnamese, some French, Spanish spoken; Visa/MasterCard/American Express/Diners Club. Excellent restaurants and super golf, tennis, scuba diving nearby.

DIRECTIONS: from Rte. 1 exit at Ocean Ave. and turn left at 2nd stop sign onto Junipero. Inn is 2 blocks down on right.

The Farmhouse guest house.

MISSION RANCH

Saved and restored by Clint Eastwood

Mission Ranch is perhaps best known for the fact that it was saved from demolition by Clint Eastwood, who is now its owner. Situated next to the Carmel Mission, the Ranch was a potato farm in the 1850's and then a working dairy ranch until opening its doors to guests in 1937. All of the original, white clapboard buildings—the Creamery, Farmhouse, Bunkhouse and Hay Loft—were refurbished in 1992 and now comprise the guest quarters.

Aside from its famous proprietor, Mission Ranch is most notable for its serene setting. A sizable spread, it sits on a bluff overlooking a vast, green pasture of grazing sheep and the distant ocean. Towering eucalyptus, cypress trees, and Monterey pines

Left above, the Meadowview rooms. Below, the restaurant looks toward the water.

shade the grounds and various cottages. It's a wonderful place to just sink into an Adirondack chair and soak in the Old California atmosphere. The view is so splendid, some guests come here just to paint the scenery.

Though the guest buildings vary widely in their configurations, their interiors all have a tasteful, yet no-frills theme, with patchwork quilts and American country furnishings. The most interesting are the Farmhouse, Hay Loft, and Meadowview rooms. There is also a Honeymoon Cottage, built in 1900, which was once used in the film "Summer Place."

Breakfast is served in the clubhouse near the tennis courts. The Mission Ranch Restaurant, which is open to the public for informal dinners, is a popular watering hole for locals and visitors alike.

MISSION RANCH, 26270 Dolores St., Carmel, CA 93923; (800) 538-8221; (408) 624-6436; Fax (408) 626-4163. Open all year. Thirty-one rooms, not all with private baths. Rates: $85 to $225, including deluxe continental breakfast. Inquire about children; no smoking; no pets; Visa/MasterCard/American Express. Tennis courts on premises. Carmel State Beach, Carmel Mission, and golf courses nearby. Mission Ranch Restaurant, Rio Grill, and Mondos recommended for dining.

DIRECTIONS: from Hwy. 1, turn west on Rio Rd., then left on Lasuen Dr. (at Carmel Mission).

The inn is now owned by Doris Day and partners.

CYPRESS INN

A Carmel landmark since 1929

The white Spanish façade of the Cypress Inn has been a Carmel landmark since its opening in 1929. With thirty-four guest rooms it could be categorized as a small hotel, but the congenial staff and unique amenities give the inn a homelike atmosphere.

Co-owned by actress and animal rights activist Doris Day, the Cypress Inn welcomes pets with open arms—a policy which draws a high percentage of repeat guests. It's not unusual to see people strolling in and out of the lobby with dogs of all sizes. Upon arrival, animals are greeted with dog biscuits, special beds, and other pet pamperings. As it is forbidden to leave dogs or cats alone in the rooms, pet sitters

Left, one of the guests enjoying the sitting room.

are also available. In the wood-beamed living room is a thick photo album showing all the furry friends who have visited the inn.

Of the rather conventionally-decorated bedrooms, the Tower Room is most unique. From the living room you climb a spiral staircase to the bedroom which is within the main tower of the building. It's a snug room with skylights, book nooks, original tilework, and a nice view of Carmel. All of the rooms are equipped with telephones, televisions, a decanter of sherry and the daily newspaper. Every morning a continental breakfast is served either in the small bar (where Doris Day movie posters hang on the walls) or in a pretty garden courtyard. Downtown Carmel, one of the most enchanting towns on the Pacific coast, is right outside the door.

CYPRESS INN, Lincoln & 7th Sts., PO Box Y, Carmel, CA 93921; (800) 443-7443; (408) 624-3871; Fax (408) 624-8216; Dennis LeVett, Terry Melcher, and Doris Day, owners; Hollace Thompson, gen'l manager. Open all year. Thirty-four rooms, all with private baths. Rates: $95 to $245, including continental breakfast; each pet $17 extra. Children welcome with advance notice; 16 nonsmoking rooms; Spanish spoken; pets welcome; all credit cards accepted. Weddings can be arranged. Carmel Mission, beach, shops, and galleries all within walking distance. Mondo's, Flying Fish Grill, and Roys (at Spanish Bay) recommended for dining.

DIRECTIONS: from Hwy. 1, exit at Ocean Ave. Turn left on Lincoln St. and proceed 1 block.

Guests in this room are enthralled by the view.

MARTINE INN

Ocean front villa

The luxury and beauty of the Monterey Peninsula can be found at this pink-stucco Mediterranean-style villa. The coastline is at the doorstep and the windows of the inn afford sweeping vistas for watching whales, sea otters, sailboat races, and crashing waves. Most of the rooms have an ocean view, but for those without that privilege, there are sitting rooms on each floor with a panoramic view.

For furnishing each guest room the Martines have selected a particular period or style and furnished them with the most remarkable pieces available, including a formal mahogany bedroom set featured at the 1869 World's Fair, and an art deco room complete with lit Coca-Cola sign. In the Early American Room there is a rare American armoire dating back to 1850 with a cherry-wood interior and bird's-eye maple surface. Two Victorian tobacco stands with copper-lined humidors serve as end tables. In another room a Captain's bed is ornamented with carved ship's wheels.

Since the days when it was home to Laura and James Parke of Parke-Davis Pharmaceuticals, gala entertaining of socialites and dignitaries has been part of the Martine Inn. The same grandeur prevails today as Marion Martine explains: "We are entertaining the same way today they would have at the turn of the century."

All of the exquisite silver and furnishings throughout the house are of museum quality. Quite impressive is the immense Sheffield silver server made in 1765 and graciously incorporated into the breakfast presentation. Adding further elegance is a rare globe-shaped Victorian repossé silver butter dish, silver coffee and tea service, and elegant Victorian china. The Martines share their signed Tiffany Loving Cup with couples celebrating weddings and anniversaries.

MARTINE INN, 255 Ocean View Boulevard, Pacific Grove, CA 93950; (408) 373-3388; Marion & Don Martine, hosts. Nineteen elegantly furnished rooms, each with private bath, several with fireplaces, several with ocean views. Rates: $125 to $230. Includes full gourmet breakfast served in dining room with spectacular view. Hors d'oeuvres and refreshments in the evening. Antique silver service used for coffee and teas. Golf, tennis, jogging path, bike path all adjacent or nearby. Four blocks from Monterey Peninsula Aquarium & Cannery Row. German, Spanish, and Italian spoken. Handicap access; Visa/MasterCard/American Express.

DIRECTIONS: from Rte. 1, take Pacific Grove/Pebble Beach exit. Follow signs to Pacific Grove. Proceed on Rte. 68, which becomes Forrest Avenue, and follow all the way to Ocean View Blvd. Take a right and go 10 blocks to the inn.

SEVEN GABLES INN

Museum-quality opulence

Filled with an impressive collection of fine art, statuary, ornamental china, and antique furnishings, the House of the Seven Gables is one of the grandest homes on the Monterey Peninsula. The result of thoughtful choices made over many decades, it is filled with pieces acquired by John and Nora Flatley during their extensive travels. Not bought to be coveted as "museum pieces," the extravagant collection is used and enjoyed by family and guests.

Whether you are discovering an eighteenth-century oil painting or marveling at the detailing on a Sèvres vase, the hosts are delighted you noticed. Six family members, who share various aspects of innkeeping, will be happy to tell you an interesting aside about a particular marble statue or piece of ornate furniture. Notice the beautiful sunset if you happen to be in the dining room. The rays bounce off a monumental crystal chandelier and reflect in a floor-to-ceiling pier mirror.

Since they became innkeepers in 1958, the Flatleys have lovingly tended the flower gardens that border their house and the imposing shoreline. Lovers' Point Beach and the sea are just steps away, and the dramatic Monterey coastline can be seen from each of the inn's twelve guest rooms. Cannery Row is a three-minute drive or a short walk along the waterfront, and the famous Seventeen-Mile Drive begins at the front door.

SEVEN GABLES INN, 555 Ocean View Boulevard, Pacific Grove, CA 93950; (408) 372-4341; The Flatley family, owners. Susan and Ed are adult family members involved with the various facets of innkeeping. Spanish, German, Greek spoken. Fourteen rooms in the main house and in several separate cottages and a carriage house, all with ocean views and full baths. Rates: $105 to $205. Includes generous light breakfast that often offers scones, quiche, muffins, etc. Children 12 and over; no pets; no smoking; Visa/MasterCard and personal checks accepted; afternoon tea served. Duke the dog in residence.

DIRECTIONS: from Highway 1 take the Pacific Grove/Pebble Beach exit. Follow the signs to Pacific Grove. Once in Pacific Grove the road becomes Forest Avenue. Stay on Forest Avenue to Ocean View Blvd., and then right two blocks to Seven Gables Inn.

Left, the house contains a collection of extraordinary antiques.

THE GATEHOUSE INN

A Bradbury & Bradbury showpiece

A short stroll from the sweeping shoreline of Monterey Bay, The Gatehouse Inn was once a haunt of John Steinbeck, who used to pay literary visits to owner Alice Langford. It is said that her husband, Senator Benjamin Langford, grew tired of looking for the keys to the front gate every evening and finally pulled the gate down—thus, its name.

The two-story Italianate Victorian has a central tower and is painted white with orange, yellow, and green trim. The interior is beautifully restored and highlighted by ornamental Bradbury & Bradbury wallpaper extending in a kaleidoscope pattern from the entry to the ceiling of the second-floor hallway. Unique, old-fashioned light fixtures cast their glow over polished wood floors and Oriental carpets in the wicker-filled parlor and dining room.

The Langford Room is the largest and lightest of the eight guest rooms. It boasts a claw foot tub and wood stove in the bedroom, with multiple windows providing an ocean view across the rooftops. The Captain's Room, in the newer annex, has an exotic, nautical flair. Several other rooms, such as Steinbeck and Otter's Cove, have their own private patios.

Guests can avail themselves of beverages in the kitchen refrigerator anytime. Afternoon tea (wine, cider, tea, sweets and crudités with dip) and a full buffet breakfast are served in the dining room. You can also relax and mingle in the crisp, wicker-filled parlor.

Left above, the ceaseless crashing of the waves on the rocky shore a block from the inn is mesmerizing. Below, the stately inn building.

Second floor hallway showing the decorative ceiling à la Bradbury & Bradbury.

THE GATEHOUSE INN, 225 Central Ave., Pacific Grove, CA 93950; (800) 753-1881; (408) 649-8436; Lois DeFord, manager. Open all year. Eight rooms, all with private baths. Rates: $110 to $150, including full breakfast and afternoon tea. Children welcome; no smoking; Spanish spoken; no pets; all credit cards accepted. The Aquarium, Cannery Row, American Tin Cannery Factory Outlets, and oceanfront recreational trail nearby. The Fish Wife, Pepper's Mexicali Cafe, and The Old Bath House recommended for dining.

DIRECTIONS: from Hwy. 1, exit at Hwy. 68/Pacific Grove. Follow Hwy. 68 to business area where it becomes Forest Ave. Turn right on Central Ave. and angle right onto 2nd St. into the inn's lefthand driveway.

The Langford Room.

The wicker-filled parlor.

GREEN GABLES

Romantic alcoves and sea views

Green Gables Inn faces the arresting shoreline of Monterey Bay in Pacific Grove. In a town once famous for its religious conferences, it is ironic that William Lacy, a prominent businessman of the 1880s, picked this spiritually conservative spot to build a house for his mistress.

The Queen Anne mansion was also the 1960s home of Roger and Sally Post, who now own a successful collection of inns in California. One of the Post Family trademarks is a profusion of amenities, and Green Gables Inn is no exception, with a full breakfast, afternoon wine and hors d'oeuvres, all-day goodies and beverages, and an evening glass of port.

The upstairs guest rooms in the main house (though mostly with shared baths) are the most romantic, with cozy alcoves and sloping ceilings. One room, which was originally a chapel, features a rib-vaulted ceiling, diamond-paned windows, and window seat with bay view. The rooms vary greatly in size, from the cozy Garret Room upstairs to a spacious downstairs suite with delft-tiled fireplace. A separate Carriage House in the rear offers more modern units with private baths, fireplaces, and televisions.

Stuffed bears, lacy Victorian knick-knacks, and an original carousel horse fill the comfortable living room; and stained-glass paneling flanks the fireplace and front door. From both the living room and dining room, bay windows look out to sea.

Watching the marine life (otters, sea lions, whales), and kayakers, is a popular pastime here. A bicycling and walking trail runs along the shore, and 'quadrupeds' (side-by-side tandem bicycles) can be rented nearby.

GREEN GABLES, 104 5th Street, Pacific Grove, CA 93950; (408) 375-2095; Roger and Sally Post, owners. Tess Arthur, manager. Open all year. Eleven rooms in main house and carriage house, 7 with private baths, 4 sharing. Rates: $100 to $160 double, including full buffet breakfast. Some restrictions on children; no pets; no smoking; Visa/MasterCard/American Express. French, Italian, Continental restaurants in area.

DIRECTIONS: take Rte. 1 to Ret. 68 west and turn right into Pacific Grove. Follow through residential and business areas to Forest. Keep on Forest to the water and turn right on Ocean Blvd. to corner of 5th.

The Chapel Room.

THE MANGELS HOUSE

Antebellum mansion

The dramatic approach along the winding road of Nisene Park indicates that this bed and breakfast is going to be special. Framed by a white picket fence, the Mangels House sits high atop a long driveway. A century-old palm tree stands sentinel in the circular drive.

The stately symmetry of the architecture, a wraparound columned porch, tall windows, and a broad stairway to a double door entrance are impressive. Built as a rural vacation home in 1886 by Claus Mangels, brother-in-law of sugar baron Claus Spreckels, the Southern style mansion is the epitome of grace and charm, down to the white fringed porch swing and wisteria ascending the porch's columns.

Jackie, the English-born innkeeper, has a marvelously fresh contemporary taste, blending modern art and country Victorian décor. The living room is so enormous that it dwarfs a grand piano. An eight-foot wide floor-to-ceiling rough-cut marble fireplace with its three-foot logs increases the imposing scale.

Mangels' lemon-hued dining room is similarly grand, its sparse majesty enhanced by a long narrow table, polished to a high gloss. The only adornment is a formal portrait of Claus Mangels behind the head of the table and portraits of his two wives on either side of the room. Because the ceilings are high, the straight staircase just inside the entry rises with dramatic elegance to the second floor bedrooms.

THE MANGELS HOUSE. 570 Aptos Creek Road, P.O. Box 302, Aptos, CA 95001; (408) 688-7982; Jacqueline and Ron Fisher, hosts. Six rooms, all with private baths. Rates: $105 to $135. Includes full breakfast of fruits and breads, omelets, casseroles, and pancakes. Spanish and French spoken. Smoking in sitting room and on porches. Children over 12; Visa/MasterCard.

DIRECTIONS: from Rte. 1 take Seacliff Beach/Aptos exit. Turn onto Soquel Drive. Proceed ⅓ mile under the RR Bridge. About 100 feet on the left, before the shopping center, take a left onto Aptos Creek Road.

The Mauve Room has a marble fireplace.

The library/salon.

The Sissinghurst Room.

INN AT DEPOT HILL

Once a railroad depot

When it comes to luxurious B&B's, it would be hard to top the Inn at Depot Hill. This 1901 railroad depot has been transformed into an exquisite inn with each of its eight guest rooms designed to evoke a different romantic locale. The Delft Room, for instance, is a study in Dutch blue and white; Sissinghurst, a traditional English-chintz garden room; the Railroad Baron is crowned by a domed ceiling, opulent red and gold fabrics, and vintage pullman appointments.

Five of the bedrooms have private patios with romantic outdoor hot tubs. Each room boasts a wood-burning fireplace, built-in stereo system, two televisions (one in the bathroom), a VCR (with a library of videos concealed in Shakespeare faux book covers in the parlor), telephone and modem, fluffy featherbed and embroidered linens, bathrobes, long-

Left, the Delft Room.

stemmed roses, and local travel literature. In the marble bathrooms are two-person showers, piles of Egyptian cotton towels, luxury soaps, a hairdryer, coffee maker, bottled water, and much more.

Wine, Italian sodas, cheeses, crackers, crudités, dip and mushroom pâte are laid out in the dining room every afternoon. After a dinner in downtown Capitola, just two blocks away, guests return to find their beds turned down, along with dessert and port. A gourmet breakfast can be delivered to your room, in the dining room, or out on the patio.

The Inn at Depot Hill is the ultimate in pampering and romance—the kind of place where you never want to leave your room.

INN AT DEPOT HILL, 250 Monterey Ave., Capitola-by-the-Sea, CA 95010; (800) 572-2632; (408) 462-3376; Fax (408) 462-3697; Suzie Lankes and Dan Floyd, owners. Open all year. Four suites and four rooms, all with luxurious private baths and some with private hot tubs on their patios. Rates: $165 to $250, including full breakfast, afternoon wine and hors d'oeuvres, and dessert. Inquire about children; smoking permitted on outside patios only; German spoken; no pets; all credit cards accepted. Beach, restaurants, shops, and galleries within walking distance. Shadowbrook, Balzac Bistro, and Stockton Bridge Grill recommended for dining.

DIRECTIONS: from Hwy. 1, on the north side of Monterey Bay, exit at Park Ave./New Brighton Beach. Proceed towards the ocean, turn left on Monterey Ave. and immediately left into driveway of inn.

A breakfast quiche.

Breakfast becomes an extraordinary experience in this room.

CLIFF CREST

Breakfasting with Mozart and Brahms

This sprightly Queen Anne is tucked into the historic area of Beach Hill, a surprisingly quiet residential community. Near the beach, board-walk, and fisherman's wharf, it was built in 1890 for a lieutenant governor of California who helped to establish Redwoods State Park.

The most dramatic feature of the house is a two-story belvedere tower. The ground floor of the tower, where breakfast is served, is enclosed by six tall windows, transforming it into a semi-circular solarium. Above each window a panel of red, purple, and blue stained glass adds festive splashes of color. Two lace-covered round tables seat eight, and because this spot is so delightful, guests are always reluctant to see breakfast end.

The second story is an open balustrade porch. Lattice work and two interior railings add an airy, garden-like mood to the interior. Guests may gaze through the living room, through the solarium and on to the secluded grassy yard and flower garden designed by John McClaren, the landscape architect of Golden Gate Park in San Francisco. The bright pink azaleas, the purple blossoms of the potato vine, and the orange bird of paradise create a vibrant range of color.

There is attention to details, from providing fresh flowers to lighting the fireplace in the evening, lending romantic touches wherever possible. Each guest receives her personally prepared restaurant guide entitled "Our Favorites." Restaurants are categorized according to those "within walking distance," those "a short drive away," and those offering "ethnic fare." The ambiance, cuisine, and price range is detailed, making it a pleasure to find a place to dine. An all-time favorite in the ethnic category, and not to be missed, is India Joze.

CLIFF CREST. 407 Cliff Street, Santa Cruz, CA 95060; (408) 427-2609; Bruce and Sharon Taylor, hosts. Five rooms, each with private bath, two with fireplaces. Rates: $85 to $135. Includes full breakfast of fresh fruits, pastries, breads, and egg dishes; evening wine and cheese. No smoking; not equipped for children; no pets; Visa/MasterCard/American Express/Discover. Two blocks from Monterey Bay.

DIRECTIONS: from Rte. 17, which becomes Ocean Street, turn right onto San Lorenzo Blvd. Proceed 3 blocks and turn left onto Riverside Drive. Go over bridge and turn right onto Third Street. At the top of the hill turn left onto Cliff Street.

BABBLING BROOK INN

Lush gardens invite romance

The Babbling Brook Inn, set picturesquely around a natural winding brook and waterfall, as a site is full of history as well. Over two-thousand years ago, the Ohlone Indians lived on these cliffs, fishing and bathing in Laurel Creek. In 1795, the mission fathers built a grist mill here, complete with a water wheel; and then in the 1870s it served as a tannery. Some actors constructed a log cabin on the mill foundations in 1909; and ultimately it expanded from a Roaring Twenties residence and writer's retreat, to a restaurant, and finally, in 1981, a bed and breakfast inn.

The surrounding pine trees give the inn a rustic, secluded ambience, but it is actually right near downtown Santa Cruz. Twelve Country French guest rooms are scattered at different levels throughout four woodsy, shingled buildings—three of them more recently-added chalets—and most enjoy private balconies and rocking chairs, wood-burning Franklin fireplaces, light pine furnishings, and tranquil garden views. Named after famous impressionist painters, many rooms display prints by such artists as Monet, Van Gogh, and Cezanne.

Guests may eat breakfast in the cheerful red and blue dining/living room, or out on a redwood sun deck among the trees. Helen King, the owner/innkeeper, is a first-rate chef and her tasty "Pookie" muffins won an award from Julia Child. She whips up such specialties as crab quiche, frittatas, and mushroom strata at breakfast. Wine and cheese are served in the afternoon, and homemade cookies are available all day.

Babbling Brook is a romantic spot for outdoor weddings, with its lush gardens, covered footbridge, tiered waterfalls, and white gazebo (purchased from a university Shakespeare production) hung with gigantic ferns. Maximum privacy and comfort is supported by a helpful, enthusiastic staff.

BABBLING BROOK INN, 1025 Laurel St., Santa Cruz, CA 95060; (408) 427-2437, Fax (408) 427-2457; Helen King, owner. Open all year. Twelve rooms with private baths, all but 1 with tubs. Rates: $85 to $165 double ($21.50 for extra person) including full breakfast. Children over 12 welcome; restricted pets; no smoking; all major credit cards accepted. Nearby are a beach and boardwalk, tennis courts, golf.

DIRECTIONS: from Rte. 1 take Laurel St. south 1½ blocks towards the ocean. Look for sign on right.

Owner Helen King in the cool shade of her garden.

NEW DAVENPORT BED & BREAKFAST INN

Spectacular coastline, special people

Just nine miles north of Santa Cruz, on Highway 1, the tiny community of Davenport resides along a magnificent stretch of California coastline. A good number of the two hundred populating the village are craftspeople (from a boat builder to a knife maker). Foremost among them are Marcia and Bruce McDougal.

After successfully operating the local Big Creek Pottery School, the McDougals opened the New Davenport Cash Store as an outlet for the school's pottery. It later evolved into a center for an outstanding selection of pottery, jewelry, textiles, and folk art from around the world. Shortly thereafter, they opened the New Davenport Restaurant, a casual establishment that offers wholesome, fine home cooking.

The New Davenport Bed and Breakfast is this energetic couple's newest addition to the community. Rooms are contemporary in design, and each is decorated with artwork and crafts. A wraparound porch on the second story of the main building is a wonderful place to relax and enjoy the beauty of the surrounding landscape.

Davenport is a great place to watch the gray whales as they migrate along the coast from February to May, because it is here they come closest to the coast. Some of the most famous wind-surfer beaches are located at Davenport and nearby.

NEW DAVENPORT BED & BREAKFAST INN. 31 Davenport Avenue, Davenport, CA 95017; (408) 425-1818 or 426-4122; Bruce and Marcia McDougal, owners. Twelve rooms; eight in two-story western-style building with a wraparound porch, four in adjacent restored home. All with private baths. Rates: $65 to $120. Includes a generous continental breakfast on weekends and a full breakfast on weekdays. Complimentary drink at bar. Children over twelve; no pets; smoking on the porches only. Visa/MasterCard/American Express.

DIRECTIONS: on Rte. 1, halfway between San Francisco and Monterey Bay. Nine miles north of Santa Cruz. Slow down when you get to Davenport and you'll see it!

All the rooms are attractive, and have stunning views.

SAN FRANCISCO BAY AREA

GOOSE & TURRETS B&B

An earth-friendly historic inn

Built in 1908, this Italianate structure served variously as town hall, post office, general store, Sunday school, and even the Spanish American War Veterans Country Club. Canons from that period still flank the entrance. Back then, the seaside village of Montara was an art colony retreat for Bohemians from San Francisco. Whether by coincidence or tradition, the Goose & Turrets B&B still has a Bohemian quality to it.

Raymond and Emily Hoche-Mong, who are also active pilots and conservationists, have been welcoming guests with their warm-hearted repartée since 1983. Their guest rooms vary from low-key to eccentric. In the Clipper Room, for instance, the walls are collaged with every aerial chart Raymond and Emily ever used. The ceiling is painted sky blue, and a propeller hangs from the wall.

But the best part of this inn is actually outdoors. The terraced garden is surrounded by a fantastic, twenty-foot-high Monterey cypress hedge, which also encloses a bocce ball court and three mascot geese who announce the arrival of every new guest with noisy honks.

Emily puts it this way: "We are a historic, earth-friendly inn catering to readers, nature-lovers, pilots and enthusiastic eaters." Her creative four-course breakfasts will certainly attest to the latter.

The Clipper Room.

A breakfast assortment.

Children welcome; smoking allowed outside only; French spoken; no pets; all credit cards accepted. Tidepooling, whale watching, winery, galleries, and aero-sightseeing nearby. Foglifter, Mezza Luna, and Chateau des Fleurs recommended for dining.

DIRECTIONS: from Hwy. 1, turn east on 2nd St., right on Main St., and left on 3rd St. (which becomes George St.), proceeding 1/2 mile.

GOOSE & TURRETS B&B, 835 George St., PO Box 937, Montara, CA 94037-0937; (415) 728-5451; Fax (415) 728-0141; Emily & Raymond Hoche-Mong, owners. Five rooms, all with private baths. Rates: $85 to $125, including four-course breakfast.

La Lluva room.

Los Nuves room.

CYPRESS INN ON MIRAMAR BEACH

Sweeping ocean panoramas

Cypress Inn on Miramar Beach shares the same owners as the swank Inn on Depot Hill, but the emphasis here is more on nature and serenity. The contemporary house is built of natural wood, and it faces a pristine, five-mile sand beach. All eight rooms have private decks with sweeping ocean panoramas. The interior, painted in earth tones, is furnished in natural pine and wicker. A dramatic skylight brings the outdoors into the three-story living room, which is highlighted by a fireplace, Mexican chairs, and whimsical, Oaxacan wood carvings. The radiant-heated terra cotta floors add to the general warmth. Owners Suzie Lankes and Dan Floyd recently added four larger, more luxurious suites to a newly acquired house next door. A conference center is also housed in this building.

Guests who have stayed at The Inn on Depot Hill will recognize some of the same luxurious amenities: feather beds, afternoon hors d'oeuvres, and a gourmet breakfast—usually featuring peaches-and-cream French toast. There is also an in-house masseuse, which is a rarity for most B&B's. Everything here is geared to complete relaxation, as the first few breaths of fresh ocean air will confirm. The main activity here consists of endless walks on the beach. This remote stretch of the San Francisco Peninsula is also one of the few remaining spots where you can still horseback ride unescorted on the beach.

Left above, the wondrous Miramar Beach. Below, the inn at the beach.

The sunlit sitting room.

CYPRESS INN ON MIRAMAR BEACH, 407 Mirada Rd., Half Moon Bay, CA 94019; (800) 832-3224; (415) 726-6002; Fax (415) 712-0380; Suzie Lankes & Dan Floyd, owners. Open all year. Twelve rooms and suites, all with private baths, fireplaces, and ocean views. Rates: $150 to $275, including full breakfast. Inquire about children; smoking permitted on outside decks only; no pets; all credit cards accepted. Five-mile beach and bike trail only steps away. Horseback riding, sea kayaking, and sailing nearby. Miramar Beach Restaurant, Moss Beach Distillery, and Shorebird in Princeton-by-the-Sea recommended for dining.

DIRECTIONS: from Hwy. 1, 30 minutes south of San Francisco, turn west on Medio Ave and proceed to the ocean.

The Rote Rose Room.

The herb garden.

SEAL COVE INN

An English country manor

Newly built to resemble an English country manor, the Seal Cove Inn enjoys a spectacular setting amid a remote twenty-acre marine reserve on the San Francisco Peninsula. Beyond the inn's garden and meadow, a long row of cypress trees frame the view, guiding the eye to the sea. A short stroll through this hauntingly beautiful grove brings you to the cliff's edge, where seals frolic in the ocean far below.

The guest rooms—five on the main level and five upstairs with cathedral ceilings—are designed to take full advantage of the view, each one having its own balcony or patio. Every country-style bedroom has a wood-burning fireplace with a plentiful supply of wood. Televisions and VCR's are hidden in armoires, and the wet bars are stocked with compli-

Left above, wine and hors d'oeuvres served in the living room. Below, the impressive inn building.

mentary wine and beverages. In the pristine, white-tiled bathrooms are terry robes, towel warmer, and heaters for the typically foggy mornings. Daily newspapers, nightly turn-down service, and afternoon wine and hot hors d'oeuvres are among the other luxuries here.

Every detail at Seal Cove Inn has been carefully thought out, due in no small part to the fact that owner Karen (Brown) Herbert is also a travel writer who has reviewed hundreds of B&B's for her own guidebook series. She and her husband Rick (who live at the inn with their two children) have taken this experience and created a superior inn that combines all of the qualities they value most at other B&B's.

SEAL COVE INN, 221 Cypress Ave., Moss Beach, CA 94038; (415) 728-4114; Fax (415) 728-4116; Karen & Rick Herbert, owners. Closed Dec. 22-25. Ten rooms, all with private baths. Rates: $165 to $250, including full breakfast in dining room (continental in guest rooms) and afternoon wine and hors d'oeuvres. Children allowed in downstairs room only; smoking permitted outside only; no pets; all credit cards accepted. Conference room available. Tidepools, park and beach walks, bike trails, and whale watching nearby. Pasta Moon, Moss Beach Distillery, and Foglifter recommended for dining.

DIRECTIONS: from Hwy. 1 in Moss Beach, turn west on Cypress Ave. (watch for the Moss Beach Distillery sign) and proceed 1/2 mile.

MILL ROSE INN

An extravagant English garden

The Mill Rose lights up its neighborhood with a profusion of natural color. Owners Eve and Terry Baldwin designed an extravagant English country garden that brightens up even the foggiest day. Their corner lot welcomes visitors with delicate coral and pink poppies, tall purple-blue delphiniums, lavender, coral alstrimeria, blue larkspur, yellow dahlias, marigolds, and hollyhocks. Not to mention approximately 200 roses.

The luxuriousness continues on the inside. Each spacious room, as Eve says, "is an adventure in elegance and comfort." Many boast dramatic hand-pulled wallpaper sets from the exclusive firm of Bradbury & Bradbury. All but one have wood-burning fireplaces—with fragrant almond wood—and every one sparks a romantic fantasy.

The attention to detail prompted one guest to remark: "You don't need to choose a room, you just need to plan a number of visits." Besides the practicalities of electric mattress pad, well-stocked mini-refrigerator, and coffee maker in the rooms, the embellishments range from Austrian moiré balloon curtains, needlework dating back to the 1860s, and silver dressing table sets to hand-thrown ceramic sinks and window boxes.

Terry's background in horticulture fits in perfectly with Eve's interior design experience. The backyard gazebo and spa, a mecca for hedonists, stands as a perfect example of their collaboration.

Breakfasts are lavish affairs as well, with warmed plates and such delicacies as baked bananas with pineapple, minted melon balls, or peach soup supplementing the hot egg dish, fresh baked goods, and homemade jams.

MILL ROSE BED AND BREAKFAST INN, 615 Mill Street, Half Moon Bay, CA 94019; (415) 726-9794, (800) 900-7673, Fax (415) 726-3031; Eve and Terry Baldwin, owners. Six beautiful rooms; all with private bath, refrigerator, telephone, and cable TV; five with fireplaces, two are suites. Rates: $165 to $265, additional person $25 per night. Includes full gourmet breakfast. Smoking on deck and in garden areas only. Older children are welcome; pets are not; Spanish and German spoken; American Express/MasterCard/Visa/Discover. Gazebo whirlpool spa on premises; bicycle rental, horseback riding, golf, tennis, and beach nearby.

DIRECTIONS: from San Francisco take Hwy. 280 or US-101 south to the Half Moon Bay exit (Hwy. 92 west). Turn left on Main St., go two blocks to Mill St. and take a right onto Mill. The house is on the right.

The Great Hall.

GARRATT MANSION

Built in the grand manner

The Garratt Mansion is situated in a quiet historic neighborhood on the island of Alameda. Built in 1893 by industrialist W.T. Garratt, the blue Colonial Revival home is distinguished by a columned porch and large bay windows. Original leaded and stained-glass windows flank the entry which opens to a wood-paneled great hall. Emanating from here are a reception room, dining room, and beautifully carved stair-case leading to two floors of bedrooms. The polished wood floors are laid with Oriental carpets, and a Medieval-like tapestry hangs on the staircase wall.

On the second level is a uniquely-built, balcony-like parlor where there are games, puzzles, refreshments, and cookies. Diana's Room is the largest and lightest bedroom, with a bamboo canopy bed, fireplace, and lots of windows. In the bathroom are inlaid hardwood floors and a claw foot tub. The Cap-

tain's Room, more masculine and nautical, has a porthole window and blue-gold starry wallpaper. The other bedrooms are furnished in homey antiques, quilts, and wicker, with nice, up-to-date showers.

Because of its location in the East San Francisco Bay, more than half of the inn's guests are business travelers. Innkeepers Royce and Betty Gladden make sure everyone is fueled for the day with a generous breakfast of fresh-squeezed orange juice, fruit, a selection of breads and a hot specialty such as a blintz soufflé with fresh fruit syrup, or a frittata with red and green pepper sauce, or "heavenly hots" pancakes with smoked chicken-and-apple sausages.

GARRATT MANSION, 900 Union St., Alameda, CA 94501; (510) 521-4779; Fax (510) 521-6796; Royce & Betty Gladden, owners. Open all year. Seven rooms; five with private baths, two with shared bath. Rates: $75 to $125, including full breakfast. Well behaved children welcome; smoking allowed outside only; no pets; all credit cards accepted. Weddings and receptions can be arranged. Alameda Museum, historic walks, and San Francisco Bay nearby. Courtyard, Chevys, and Skylight Cafe recommended for dining.

DIRECTIONS: from I-880, exit at High St. and head west onto the island of Alameda. Turn right at Central Ave., proceed 1.5 miles to Union St. and turn left.

THE MANSION AT LAKEWOOD

A rescued estate wonderfully restored

As the white electronic gates open to let your car pass through, you sense that this is going to be a luxurious treat. The gravel driveway encircles a wide fountain and stops before an elegant, white, two-story mansion, where gracious hosts Sharyn and Mike McCoy greet you with a warm smile and a cold glass of lemonade.

The Mansion at Lakewood is a lavish surprise in an otherwise quiet residential neighborhood. But, back in the 1860s, it was the only home in this area, built on two-thousand privately-owned acres. While the house was expanded to a grand scale in the early 1900s, the land was sold off, finally narrowing down to three acres.

Sharyn and Mike rescued the estate from slated subdivision, performed a miraculous transformation on the run-down mansion, and opened the inn in 1988. Today you would never guess that when they first moved in, most of the doors had been kicked in, there was no heat, and the mansion had only one working bathroom. From its expansive soft lawn outside, to its vast library, once a ballroom, and country-style living and dining rooms inside, the inn is the ultimate in polished taste.

Each of the seven exquisite bedrooms offers one delightful surprise after another. Sharyn did all the decorating, and the downstairs suits are particularly spectacular: Summerhouse features a sunny sitting room with claw-footed tub and hand-painted floors, and in the bedroom, an old vault has been cleverly converted to a walk-in closet. The Estate Suite has a high, brass, canopied bed and champagne-pink goose down comforter, spacious sitting area, private terrace and fireplace, and, best of all, an oversized sunken marble bath with Jacuzzi tub, double shower and double sinks.

THE MANSION AT LAKEWOOD, 1056 Hacienda Drive, Walnut Creek, CA 96598; (510) 945-3600; Sharyn and Mike McCoy, owners. Open all year. Five rooms with canopied and 4-poster queen beds and 2 suites with king beds, all with private baths, and one with large double shower and one with double Jacuzzi. Rates: $135 to $300; corporate rates available, including full breakfast. Children discouraged; no pets; smoking outside only; all major credit cards. Continental, Italian, French, Mexican, seafood dining in area.

DIRECTIONS: from US-101 north over Bay Bridge take Rte. 580 to Rte. 24 east at Walnut Creek sign. Exit right at Ygnacio Valley Rd. to 7th signal light at Homestead Ave. Turn right and go 1 block past 1st stop sign and turn left onto Hacienda and look for white wrought iron gates.

The Terrace Suite.

Room 24 in the Fay House.

GRAMMA'S

Very near the Berkeley campus

A commercial twist on a home-based bed and breakfast, Gramma's runs a four-building inn some seven blocks from the University of California's Berkeley campus. Guests choose from among the modern Carriage House, the bustling Main House, the quiet Garden House, and the historic Fay House, each conveying a distinctive personality.

Owner Kathy Kuhner and two partners began with restoration of the turn-of-the-century Main House, sometimes described as a "stockbroker Tudor." Built by developer John Marshall, it's a stone and half-timbered beauty that pales only in comparison to its more sedate next-door neighbor, the Fay House, also built by Marshall.

The interior of the Fay House breathes new life into jaded architectural buffs. Used mostly for weddings, celebratory affairs, and Sunday breakfasts, the downstairs boasts original arts and crafts and art nouveau light fixtures, parquet floors with an inlaid border, and beautiful geometric stained glass.

More original stained glass, including a Mother Goose panel in the old nursery, appears scattered throughout the upstairs guest rooms, which contain an eclectic mix of old and new furniture. Beds, for example, range from wicker to brass to pine four-posters.

Wine and cheese tempt guests to while away the afternoon in the Main House parlor overlooking the small garden area in back.

GRAMMA'S ROSE GARDEN INN, 2740 Telegraph Avenue, Berkeley, CA 94705; (510) 549-2145, Fax (510) 549-1085; Kathy Kuhner, owner; Kim Mock, manager. Forty rooms: eleven in the Main House, eight in the Garden House, nine in Fay House, four in the Carriage House, eight in the Cottage House, all with private baths and TVs. Rooms vary in size dramatically. Telephones and TVs available. Rates: $85 to $145. Includes expanded continental breakfast buffet and wine and cheese in the afternoon. No smoking in the common rooms. Children welcome; no pets; all major credit cards.

DIRECTIONS: from I-80 to Berkeley, take the Ashby Ave. exit, go 2 miles east to Telegraph Ave., then turn left and go 5 blocks to Ward St., where you'll find a back parking lot.

Epiphania's Room.

CAPTAIN WALSH HOUSE

Stunningly decorated

The Captain Walsh House is, without a doubt, the most creatively decorated inn in California. Built in 1849 as a wedding present for General M.G. Vallejo's daughter, Epiphania, the home was lovingly renovated by architect Reed Robbins and her husband Steve. An engaging, energetic couple, they tackled everything themselves—refurnishing, elaborate hand-painting, sewing, and all of the interior design. The transformation is truly exciting—sumptuously romantic, boldly original, and, as Reed herself describes it, just plain "quirky."

In the main parlor, for example, Medieval-style curtains hang askance against tall Gothic windows. Rich, ivory-colored fabrics are piled high on the tables, while contrasting against this creamy background are amusingly dark, moody Gothic details, such as gargoyles, candelabras and church remnants. Upstairs, in golden, light-filled Epiphania's Room,

Left, the main salon.

a splendidly-canopied bed sits before a Gothic window in the center of the high-ceilinged room with its pillows piled seven layers deep. Screened off from the bed is a twenty-four-carat gold claw foot tub which springs straight from the pages of *Alice in Wonderland.*

Though all five bedrooms are filled with surprises, the most imaginative is the Library, a cozy hideaway which is surrounded by bookshelves, goofy trophies, and a real stuffed animal. The bed, which is concealed behind a wall of faux-painted, cryptically-entitled books, is folded out in the evening. A zebra-skin rug hangs from the angled ceiling of the reading loft which is accessed via a ladder. Despite the humor, everything—from the formal, gourmet breakfast to their elaborate weddings—is executed with the utmost taste.

CAPTAIN WALSH HOUSE, 235 East L St., Benicia, CA 94510; (707) 747-5653; Fax (707) 747-6265; Reed & Steve Robbins, owners. Open all year. Five rooms, all with private baths. Rates: $110, including full gourmet breakfast and afternoon wine. Children allowed, though rooms are double occupancy only; smoking permitted outside only; no pets (Bill, a clumber spaniel is in residence with his cat); all credit cards accepted. Weddings can be arranged. Camel Barn Museum, glass blowers studio, antique shops, sailing and biking nearby. First St. Foods, Mabel's and Union Hotel recommended for dining.

DIRECTIONS: from I-780, exit at East 2nd St./Central Benicia. Turn left on East 2nd St., then left on L St.

SAN FRANCISCO

VICTORIAN INN ON THE PARK

A superb location

Directly across from the verdant expanse of Golden Gate Park, the Victorian Inn on the Park best evokes turn-of-the-century San Francisco. Innkeepers Lisa and William Benau's splendid Queen Anne-style inn was built in Queen Victoria's diamond jubilee year, 1897, and it supports one of the last remaining belvedere towers in the city.

The interior décor, courtesy of Lisa's mother, Shirley Weber, has an authentic nineteenth-century feel, with velvet bedspreads, William Morris wallpaper, and love seats. The Clunie Room, in shades of light blue and burgundy, is one of the most popular guest rooms, with a gas fireplace and Victorian-style bath. From the Belvedere Room, French doors open to a third-floor balustraded porch within the open belvedere tower that overlooks the park. Behind another set of stained-glass doors is a spacious, tiled, shower-tub. The Redwood Room, with its warm paneling and working fireplace framed by original tiles, is another favorite.

With advance notice, Lisa and Bill will present

a chilled bottle of champagne to their newly arrived guests. For the business traveler, the library is equipped with a large desk, and meetings or business luncheons are easily accommodated.

VICTORIAN INN ON THE PARK, 301 Lyon Street, San Francisco, CA 94117; (415) 931-1830; (800) 435-1967; Fax (415) 931-1830; Lisa and William Benau, hosts. Twelve rooms, each with private bath. Rates: $99 to $164. Includes continental breakfast of fresh fruits and cheese, baked breads, and croissants. Children welcome; no pets; smoking is allowed with consideration to the preferences of other guests; all major credit cards accepted.

DIRECTIONS: from US-101 north, exit at Fell Street and proceed on Fell approximately 9/10ths of a mile to Lyon Street.

A guest room.

JOHN SWAIN

The Queen Anne Room.

SPENCER HOUSE

A jewel
on display

The Spencer House is a well-kept secret in the heart of San Francisco's free-spirited Haight-Ashbury district, of 1960s hippie fame. There is no identifying sign outside, the owners do not have brochures, their phone number is unlisted, and they do not advertise. After seeing the inside of this fabulous Queen Anne mansion, you will agree that there is no need to—word of mouth is enough.

Barbara and Jack Chambers spent two years carefully refurbishing the exquisite 1887 house, which had been run down by neglect. Traveling to England and France, they garnered some of the finest fabrics and antiques to be found at any inn. In the corner of the carved oak foyer stands a lovely grandfather clock, of which only one other exists. Stained glass, 18th and 19th century portraits, inlaid

wood floors, sterling silver displays, and overstuffed velvet couches all make this feel like a European house that you would pay to tour. You could be in a Loire Valley chateau.

The six upstairs guest rooms have handsome private baths, and are splendidly decorated with Persian rugs, padded wall coverings, chintz and lace curtains, elaborately-carved headboards, and original Vaseline globe light fixtures. The inviting feather beds have plump, fluffy mattresses, comforters, and pillows you can literally sink into.

Guests are often lured into the huge kitchen, a "must-see", with its scads of copper pots hanging from the ceiling, by the scent of freshly-made coffee cakes and pies. Breakfast is a formal, three to four course, candle-lit affair, served at a long dining room table that is elegantly set with sterling silver and white linen.

SPENCER HOUSE. 1080 Haight Street, San Francisco, CA 94117; (415) 626-9205, Fax (415) 626-9230; Barbara Chambers, owner. Open all year. Six rooms with private baths and double, queen, or king beds. Rates: $105 to $165, including full breakfast. No pets (as two dogs and a macaw parrot already reside at the inn); no smoking; Visa/MasterCard/American Express.

DIRECTIONS: from US-101 north, exit at Fell Street. After 1 mile, turn left on Baker Street. The inn is on the left at the corner of Baker and Haight Streets.

Left. Washington Square and the cathedral, which the front guest rooms of the inn overlook.

One of the guest rooms.

WASHINGTON SQUARE INN

Surrounded by great restaurants

Situated in San Francisco's colorful North Beach, the Washington Square Inn is a perfect place to unwind after a day of city business or sightseeing. A generous afternoon tea of crisp cucumber sandwiches, smoked salmon rolls, cheese, pâté, crackers, wine, and other refreshments awaits guests in the comfortable lobby. In colder weather, you can sink into down-filled couches and warm your feet before a crackling fireplace.

The Washington Square Inn is decorated in understated elegance by designer Nan Rosenblatt, who has owned the inn with her husband, Norm, for nearly fifteen years. Guest rooms are painted in soft pastel colors and furnished with English and French antiques, floral curtains, bedspreads, and paintings. Rooms 7 and 8, both with large bay windows facing the park and its lovely cathedral, have long, inviting window seats.

The inn's friendly staff provides the extras of a small hotel such as valet parking, baggage carried to your room, terry robes, generous fruit baskets, and evening turn-down service with chocolates placed on the pillow. Breakfast can be enjoyed in bed or at the breakfast table in the downstairs lobby.

Washington Square is in the heart of a wonderful Italian-Chinese neighborhood where some of the best restaurants in San Francisco can be found. If the smell of roasting coffee doesn't draw you into a nearby café, then the heady aroma of garlic surely will. Chinatown is a short stroll away, Coit Tower is around the corner, and you can easily catch the cable car to Union Square or Fisherman's Wharf.

In the morning you will arise to find hundreds of Chinese people practicing their *t'ai chi* exercises in the park—a memorable, mesmerizing sight. If you are tempted to join them, go ahead—many of the inn's bolder guests have been known to do just that!

WASHINGTON SQUARE INN, 1660 Stockton Street, San Francisco, CA 94133; (800) 388-0220, (415) 981-4220, Fax (415) 397-7242; Nan and Norm Rosenblatt, owners; Brooks Bayly, manager. Open all year. Fifteen rooms, 11 with private baths, 4 with shared baths. Rates: $85 to $180, including expanded continental breakfast and afternoon tea. Children accepted; no pets; inn is entirely non-smoking; all major credit cards. Valet parking for extra charge. Buca Giovanni, Amelio's and Moose's recommended for dining.

DIRECTIONS: from US-101 take Van Ness Avenue north to Union Street and turn right. Turn left on Stockton Street at Washington Square.

Owners Marily and Robert Kavanaugh, the originators of bed and breakfast in San Francisco.

THE BED AND BREAKFAST INN

Enduring British charm

Driving along Union Street, it is easy to miss Charlton Court, a narrow cul-de-sac where The Bed and Breakfast Inn is tucked away. Once found, it is like entering a South Kensington mews—two connecting Victorian buildings with white trim and red geraniums in the window boxes; delicately flowered wallpaper and paned windows; and breakfast tables set with Battenburg lace, English china, and cow creamers.

This was San Francisco's first bed and breakfast, and is still owned by Robert and Marily Kavanaugh, pioneers of the small city inn. Fifteen years ago, they found a winning formula—a caring staff, intimate surroundings, and British-style charm—which has resulted in a steady, long-time following.

Four bedrooms with shared baths occupy the Main House, as well as a penthouse flat which boasts a huge living room, kitchen, balcony, and tiny spiral staircase to the bedroom loft. Next door, at Two Charlton, are charming rooms with private baths.

Bedrooms vary greatly in size and theme, and the furnishings are informally eclectic. The Mandalay Suite suggests the Pacific, with bamboo and wicker furnishings, and The Celebrations Room features Laura Ashley fabrics and a large sunken bathtub, making it a romantic favorite.

Continental breakfast, sherry, and fruit baskets are included. To the rear, a sun deck has tables and umbrellas; and the downstairs library offers television, games, and books. Marily's flowery paintings, many of which are for sale, hang about the inn.

Guests love the way the inn is safely set back from the noise of the city, but is still so close to the trendy boutiques and cafés of Union Street. It's tempting to leave your car in a nearby garage, and walk everywhere from here. Cable cars are less than eight blocks away.

THE BED AND BREAKFAST INN, Four Charlton Court, San Francisco, CA 94123; (415) 921-9784; Robert and Marily Kavanaugh, owners; Frankie Stone, manager. Open all year. Two suites with private baths and 9 guest rooms, 7 with private baths and 2 sharing. Rates: $70 to $275, including continental breakfast in all except The Garden Suite. Children not encouraged; no pets; smoking permitted; French and Spanish spoken; no credit cards; personal checks accepted. Bonta and Pane e Vino recommended for dining nearby.

DIRECTIONS: from US-101 north take Van Ness Avenue to Union Street and turn left; turn left again on Charlton Court.

soft, flowered wallpaper, quilted bed spreads, and antique and reproduction furniture. All but eight have switch-on fireplaces. Hand-written welcome notes, fresh flowers, evening turn-down service, and the *San Francisco Chronicle* are daily amenities.

Petite Auberge, meaning "little inn", is part of the Four sisters collection—whose trademark is a surfeit of amenities. Kim Post Watson, one of the "four sisters" who oversees the inns, says that her family's goal is to combine the service of a large hotel with the intimacy of an inn. Their recipe for success: "We've developed inns that *we* would want to stay in."

PETITE AUBERGE

Provençal ambience

At Petite Auberge, you get the best of both worlds— all the trappings of a French country-inn and the heart of the city. Terra cotta tiles, crisp Pierre Deux fabrics, lace curtains, and light furnishings enhance its Provençal ambience, yet San Francisco's Union Square is less than four blocks away.

Originally built as a hotel in 1919, the narrow, five-story building displays a Baroque façade with curved bay windows. A carousel horse, winsome teddy bears, and a basket of homemade cookies greet you in the foyer. Classical music and the light scent of potpourri fill the air. Your car is whisked away by a valet, and from then on you tend to forget you are in the middle of the city.

A lovely downstairs lounge, dining area, and flower-filled patio set a cheery stage for the buffet breakfast, afternoon happy hour, and all-day beverages. Guests can sit before the fireplace and nibble on spinach feta triangles and vegetables with dill dip, while sipping wine and deciding where to dine, among San Francisco's many tantalizing restaurants.

The twenty-six guest rooms, varying in size, are impeccably furnished in French country-décor—

GRANT HUNTINGTON PHOTOGRAPH

PETITE AUBERGE, 863 Bush Street, San Francisco, CA 94108; (415) 928-6000, (800) 365-3004, Fax (415) 775-5717; Celeste Lytle, gen'l mgr. Open all year. Twenty-six rooms with private baths, 18 with gas fireplaces. Rates: $110 to $160 per room; 1 suite $220. Includes full gourmet breakfast served buffet style. Children welcome (under 5 free); no pets; no smoking; Visa/MasterCard/American Express. One block to cable cars, 3 blocks to Union Sq., 4 to Chinatown.

DIRECTIONS: go east on Bush St. to no. 863.

ALAMO SQUARE INN

A grand era revived

The inn consists of two houses on the square.

Wayne Corn, who was raised in North Carolina, and Klaus May, a native of Germany's Rhineland, make this the pleasant place it is. Innkeeper Wayne's brand of southern hospitality and resident-chef Klaus's European-style breakfasts herald the revival of that elegant era when continental-style accommodations and gracious service were commonplace.

The inn consists of two houses. One is an 1895 blend of Queen Anne and Neo-Classical Revival with a grand staircase with hand-carved balusters, a stained-glass skylight, and large parlors harking back to an era when luxurious space was fashionable. Wainscoting, rich oak floors, and elegant furnishings blend with an eclectic collection of treasures from Afghanistan, India, Iran, and China.

The adjacent house is a classic 1896 California Craftsman, and is connected to the main house by a glass-covered solarium planted with lush greenery.

ALAMO SQUARE INN, 719 Scott Street, San Francisco, CA 94117; (415) 922-2055; (800) 345-9888; FAX (415) 931-1304; Wayne Morris Corn, host; Klaus May, resident chef. Fourteen rooms, all with private baths, decorated in period pieces with oriental influence. Rates: $85 to $275. Includes hearty breakfast of omelets, breads, fruits, and fresh-squeezed orange juice. Special dinners, weddings, and conferences by arrangement. Children welcome; no pets; smoking in the solarium only; Visa/MasterCard/American Express.

DIRECTIONS: located on the west side of Alamo Square, ten blocks west of the Civic Center and two blocks north of Fell Street.

Sumptuous parlors blend Victorian and Oriental appointments.

The second-floor hallway and staircase.

ARCHBISHOP'S MANSION

Where bed and breakfast achieves eminence

Quite simply, this is the most spectacular place to stay in San Francisco. Built for the archbishop of San Francisco in 1904, it survives today for the pleasure of its guests. The original three-story open staircase, with carved mahogany columns, soars upward to a sixteen-foot stained-glass dome. The expansive entry, hallways, and large rooms are characteristic of the Second French Empire style and suggest a grand country manor. Magnificently carved mantelpieces adorn eighteen fireplaces throughout the house, and high arched windows reflect the grandeur of its era.

Whatever has frayed with the passage of time has been restored with integrity. The resplendent painted ceiling in the parlor is fashioned after the decorative detail of a nineteenth-century Aubusson carpet. A palatial environment is created by the blending of Belle Epoque furnishings with Victorian and Louis XIV statuary, paintings, and bronze chandeliers.

Because the city opera house is only six blocks away, all of the guest rooms are named after romantic operas such as Madame Butterfly, La Traviata, and Romeo and Juliet. The Don Giovanni Suite, with its grand parlor and imposing French bed, overlooks the lawns of Alamo Square. The Carmen Room is favored for its luxurious bath—a claw-foot tub which stands in front of a carved wood fireplace. La Tosca is loved for its romantic ambience.

For guests attending concerts at the Davis Symphony Hall or opera house, limousine service for special evenings is provided.

A continental breakfast is brought to your room, and the evening wine hour is accompanied by a Bechstein player piano which was once owned by Noel Coward.

THE ARCHBISHOP'S MANSION, 1000 Fulton Street, San Francisco, CA 94117; (800) 543-5820; (415) 563-7872; Rick Janvier, manager. Open all year. Fifteen rooms, all with private baths. Eleven rooms have fireplaces, several are full suites with sitting rooms. Rates: $129 to $385, including expanded continental breakfast and wine hour. Children accepted; no pets; smoking is restricted to designated common area; Visa/MasterCard/American Express. Off-street parking for eight cars and easy street parking. The public rooms are available to guests for cocktail parties, conferences, and weddings.

DIRECTIONS: on northeast corner of Alamo Square at Steiner and Fulton. Alamo Square is 8 block west of the Civic Center and 3 blocks north of Fell Street.

A Superior Suite.

INN AT THE OPERA

A haven for celebrities

Because of its prime location in the heart of the Performing Arts Center in San Francisco, the Inn at the Opera draws scores of music lovers and famous performers. Luciano Pavarotti, Placido Domingo, Mikhail Baryshnikov, Twyla Tharp, and Bobby McFerrin are just a few of the many noted names who have registered here.

Built in 1927, the narrow, seven-story hotel was renovated in 1986 at a cost of $7 million. Ranging from very small bedrooms to two-room suites, the guest quarters are decorated in soft pastels with European reproduction furnishings and half-canopied beds. Televisions are discreetly concealed inside antique armoires, while classical music wafts from the clock radios. Hand-written welcome notes, fresh flowers, a basket of red apples, terry robes, and mini bars are provided in every room. Evening turn-down

Left above, the War Memorial Opera House. Below, the Act IV Restaurant at the inn.

service is accompanied by fresh-baked cookies.

Downstairs, the lobby is appointed in soft peach and green silk and damask chairs. A hallway, lined with 1874 Paul Renouard sketches depicting scenes from the Paris Opera Ballet, leads to the inn's restaurant. Act IV is an exquisitely appointed dining room and bar. Wood paneling, richly tapestried walls, leather chairs, striking flower arrangements, soft lighting, and live piano music create an intimate, clublike setting for lunch, dinner (a sample entrée—lightly smoked sturgeon with seared salmon-spring leek tartare) or delectable, post-concert desserts. Guests of the inn enjoy a generous buffet breakfast here, complete with cheeses, meats, and egg dishes.

INN AT THE OPERA, 333 Fulton St., San Francisco, CA 94102; (800) 325-2708; (415) 863-8400; Fax (415) 861-0821; Thomas R. Noonan, owner/manager. Open all year. Forty-six rooms and suites, all with private baths. Rates: $125 to $265, including continental breakfast. Children over 12 welcome; smoking allowed; Spanish, French, and Italian spoken; no pets; all credit cards accepted. Performing Arts Center, government buildings, and neighborhood shopping nearby. Tickets to performances can be arranged through the inn. Act IV, Stars, Ivy's, and Aqua recommended for dining.

DIRECTIONS: from US-101 north, exit at 9th St./Civic Center. Follow 9th St. to Market St. and cross the street to continue on Hayes St. Turn right on Franklin St., then left at Fulton St. Valet parking available.

GOLD COUNTRY

The Lord Byron Room.

Poet's Refuge living room.

AMBER HOUSE

Poet's refuge; artist's retreat

Situated in a nice, tree-lined neighborhood only minutes from the State Capitol, Amber House consists of two side-by-side houses whose façades are like night and day. The main house, called Poet's Refuge, is a 1905 brown Craftsman-style home highlighted by stained-glass windows, a comfortable living room, and snug little library nook. All of the tastefully-decorated rooms in this house are named after poets such as Lord Byron, Chaucer, and Wordsworth. Artist's Retreat, next door, is a white 1913 Mediterranean home with columns and coved ceilings accenting the pastel-furnished living room. Here, there are four more nicely-furnished guest rooms, each named after famous artists.

Because the Amber House hosts so many business travelers, their amenities are above the norm for most inns. Every room has a private phone with voice mail, television with free movie channels, VCR, early morning coffee and newspaper outside your door, fresh-baked welcome cookies, terry robes, bottled water, and afternoon wine and sherry. Breakfast, which can be delivered to your room at any time, might consist of baked grapefruit, cheese blintzes in raspberry-peach melba sauce, sausages and muffins—all beautifully presented. The bathrooms are marvelous, with large, marble Jacuzzi tubs. The Van Gogh Room boasts a heart-shaped Jacuzzi tub for two and wicker chaise longue in its spacious, marble-floored, solarium.

With all its luxuries, the Amber House is not just a comfortable refuge for business people—it would appeal equally to romantics as well.

AMBER HOUSE, 1315 22nd St., Sacramento, CA 95816; (800) 755-6526; (916) 444-8085; Fax (916) 552-6529; Michael Richardson, owner. Open all year. Nine rooms, all with private baths (seven with Jacuzzis for two) and one with fireplace. Rates: $89 to $199, including full gourmet breakfast. Maximum two persons per room; smoking allowed on outside veranda only; no pets; all credit cards accepted. State Capitol, Convention Center, Sutter's Fort, Old Sacramento, State Railroad Museum, and Crocker Art Museum nearby.

DIRECTIONS: eight blocks east of the Capitol, between Capitol Ave. and N. St.

Left, the bathroom of the Van Gogh Room.

Your hosts, Jane and Sanford Grover.

OAK HILL RANCH

Keeping Victorian traditions alive

The opening scenes of *Little House on the Prairie* were shot within a mile of this yellow ranch house. No TV fictions here: the rolling hills, grazing cattle, and good clean air are a way of life in this part of the country.

The ranch reflects the tireless determination of its hosts, Sanford and Jane Grover, who twenty-five years ago began collecting Victorian turn posts, balconies, railings, mantelpieces, doorways, and other turn-of-the-century relics that could be salvaged and incorporated into their recently built home. The result—a replica of a turn-of-the-century ranch house that is open, spacious, and airy.

The sophisticated country breakfast reflects Sanford and Jane's interest in gourmet food. Eggs Fantasia, baked with layered scallions, peppers, and fresh mushrooms, and Crêpe Normandy filled with chunky apple sauce and brandied raisins, are house specialties.

Devoted to Victorian traditions, Sanford remains active in the Horseless Carriage Club of America, of which he was president and board member for eleven years, and Jane, on occasion, loves to dress in period clothing. They always have at least one antique car. Both are active in community affairs, especially at the regional museum, which preserves the mining, logging, and railroad histories of the area.

Surrounded by fifty-six acres at the end of a long country lane, Oak Hill Ranch is everyone's ideal western farmhouse.

OAK HILL RANCH, 18550 Connally Lane, P.O. Box 307, Tuolumne, CA 95379; (209) 928-4717. Sanford and Jane Grover, hosts. Four bedrooms with two shared and two private baths in main house, plus a private cottage with kitchen, living room, and fireplace ideal for honeymooners or families. Rates: $70 to $85. Cottage $115. Includes a full country breakfast that is a delightful event. Children over fourteen; no pets; smoking on the outside porches and decks only; no credit cards. Close to Yosemite National Park.

DIRECTIONS: from Rte. 108, take Tuolumne Rd. to Carter St. Follow Carter St. south to the schoolyard and turn left onto Elm St. Take a right onto Apple Colony Rd. The sign for Oak Hill is on the left and will point you to Connally Lane. Proceed to the end of the lane.

The inn building, nestled amid fragrantly mature gardens.

SUTTER CREEK INN

A pioneer of bed and breakfast

When Jane Way opened the Sutter Creek Inn back in 1966, renting rooms and providing breakfast for $12.50 a night, bed and breakfasts were still unknown west of the Mississippi. Situated in the center of quaint Sutter Creek, the lush, shady grounds contain an 1856 New England-style house and several outbuildings (wood shed, carriage house, storage shed) that have been converted to guest quarters.

The bedrooms are furnished in a rather funky mixture of gold rush antiques and 60s décor. Nine rooms have fireplaces, and four feature unusual swinging beds (the mattresses hang from the ceiling by chains)—an idea Jane got while vacationing in Mexico.

Long plant tables are set for a family breakfast in the country-style kitchen, where guests enjoy such treats as brown Betty and eggs, cream cheese, and capers over muffins.

Somewhat of a legend among innkeepers, Jane is not only still running the inn with her enlarged staff, but has expanded from four rooms to nineteen. Mindful about keeping the inn affordable, especially for single travelers and senior citizens, she still offers some surprisingly low-priced rooms.

Jane also does palm reading and handwriting analysis for guests. She warns that people may not like what she has to say about their handwriting, but that hasn't stopped them from lining up for a reading.

SUTTER CREEK INN, 75 Main Street, P.O. Box 385, Sutter Creek, CA 95685; (209) 267-5606; Jane Way, owner and innkeeper. Open all year. Eighteen rooms with private baths, 9 with fireplaces. Rates: $50 (double) Sun. to Thurs., $88 to $115 (double) Fri., Sat., holidays; $5 less for single. Includes hot breakfast served family-style, with complete change of menu daily. Children over 15 preferred; no pets; no smoking in rooms; no credit cards. Fine restaurants within walking distance. Town has distinctive shops and galleries. Inn has extensive gardens, large library, piano, and tapes. Handwriting analysis, foot reflexology.

DIRECTIONS: Sutter Creek is on Rte. 49 and inn is on main street in center of town.

Owners Melisande Hubbs and Patricia Cross.

The garden as it looks from the balcony.

THE HEIRLOOM

Southern graciousness

Though situated in the Sierra foothills, The Heirloom looks every bit the Southern belle. A long gravel driveway leads to the red brick mansion with its white balconies and columns facing Sutter Creek. Built in 1863 by a settler from Virginia, the home is surrounded by century-old trees, lawns, and lovely gardens.

Patricia Cross and Melisande Hubbs opened The Heirloom in 1980. Their family furnishings and heirlooms blend well together in the large living room, where various groupings of sofas, chairs, games, and books provide comfortable niches for guests.

The four guest rooms in the main house are named and decorated after the seasons. Spring has a second-floor wisteria-covered balcony overlooking the gar-

Left above, the living room. Below, the Winter Room.

den and an old magnolia tree. Autumn and Winter share a balcony with a view of the expansive lawn and its blooming flowers. Nearby, in complete contrast to this delicate mansion is a newer rammed-earth cottage with sixteen-inch-thick walls and a sod roof. Its two rooms are decorated in Early American and Early California styles, with wood-burning stoves and interiors built of pine, cedar, and redwood.

Breakfast can be served in bed, on the veranda, in the fireside dining room, or out in the garden. Fresh-squeezed orange juice is followed by seasonal fruit, two kinds of breads, and an entrée such as crêpes, soufflés, or eggs Benedict. Melisande and Patricia often greet their guests in matching, old-fashioned costumes.

THE HEIRLOOM, 214 Shakeley Lane, Ione, CA 95640; (209) 274-4468; Melisande Hubbs & Patricia Cross, owners. Closed Thanksgiving, Christmas Eve, and Christmas Day. Four rooms in main house and two rooms in adobe cottage; four with private baths, two with shared bath. Rates: $60 to $97, including full breakfast. Children over ten allowed; smoking permitted outside only; no pets; Visa/MasterCard/American Express. Gold country historic sites, wineries, antiques, fishing, and golf nearby. Teresa's Italian, The Imperial Hotel recommended for dining.

DIRECTIONS: situated west of Hwy. 49, midway between Lake Tahoe and Yosemite. Turn left on Main St., right on Preston, and left on Shakeley Lane.

The downstairs Suite in the main house.

THE AMERICAN RIVER INN

A century of hospitality

The American River Inn would be a fun place to visit for Christmas. The parlor and breakfast room are decked out in red, green, and a potpourri of Scottish and patriotic American styles. Red-uniformed toy soldiers stand at attention on the fireplace mantle and the adjoining gift shop is filled to the brim with dolls, stuffed animals, and a big Christmas tree. Accessible only via a winding, forested, fifteen-mile road, the Inn also provides a semi-alpine setting among the Ponderosa pines.

Bedrooms at the inn are reminiscent of the gold rush era, with period wallpaper, feather beds and antiques. Guest quarters are housed in three buildings, including the original turn-of-the-century hotel and two newer annexes. All are built on rambling grounds with fruit trees, a dove aviary, hammocks, badminton and croquet, bicycles, a natural rock swimming pool, and a spa. The Queen Anne House is a popular wedding and conference site, having

its own self-sufficient living room, kitchen, and five bedrooms (including a lacy honeymoon suite with a fireplace and oversized tub).

A typical breakfast includes coffee, juice, muffins, pancakes with baked apples and whipped cream, ham, and fruit, attractively presented on Royal Doulton china. In the early evening, wine, cheese, and crackers are available in the parlor or out on the deck.

The hotel has been the center of Georgetown's social life for more than a century, once operating as a gold miner's boarding house. Indeed, one miner has apparently decided to stay on permanently, as a ghost. In fact, so many guests have claimed to see "Oscar" in Room Five that owners Will and Maria Collin have even brought a spiritualist up here to check things out.

THE AMERICAN RIVER INN. Orleans St., P.O. Box 43, Georgetown, CA 95634; (916) 333-4499, (800) 245-6566, Fax (916) 333-9253; Will and Maria Collin, owners. Open all year. 25 rooms and suites in 3 buildings, with 14 in main house with private and shared baths. Rates: $85 to $115 double, including full breakfast in dining room or on patio. Children over 9 welcome; no pets; smoking allowed; all major credit cards. Croquet, badminton, ping pong, horseshoes, putting green, driving range, pool, Jacuzzi, mountain bikes on property. Rafting, kyaking, fishing, biking, gold panning, ballooning nearby.

DIRECTIONS: from Sacramento take either Rte. 50 or 80 to Rte. 49 and follow signs to Georgetown, where inn is at corner of Main Street and Orleans.

The Cottage Suite.

COLOMA INN

Make yourself at home

Nestled in the heart of the Marshall Gold Discovery State Park is The Coloma Country Inn, a pretty farmhouse built in 1852. Its quiet, country setting is picture-perfect: Horse-drawn carriages clop past the white picket fence; in back, the hill slopes up from a garden gazebo and duck pond to a steepled church; surrounding all of this are the rolling Sierra Nevada foothills.

The farmhouse has five comfy bedrooms furnished with innkeeper Cindi Ehrgott's lifelong collection of antiques and handmade patchwork quilts. Guests can relax in wingback chairs before the living room fireplace, make themselves at home in the kitchen, and pretty much have the house to themselves, since the owners live in another house nearby. Two additional suites with kitchens are in an adjacent carriage house, providing even more privacy. The fresh white-and-red Geranium Suite has its own patio enclosed by latticework, grape vines and wisteria.

THE COLOMA COUNTRY INN, 345 High St., PO Box 502, Coloma, CA 95613; (916) 622-6919; Alan & Cindi Ehrgott, owners. Open all year. Five rooms in main house and two suites (one with two bedrooms) in carriage house, all with private baths. Rates: $89 to $99, including full breakfast. Children welcome; smoking allowed outside only; Spanish spoken; no pets; no credit cards. Bicycles available. Whitewater rafting, hot-air ballooning, gold panning, historic points of interest, and wine tasting all within walking distance. Zachary Jack's and Vineyard House recommended for dining.

DIRECTIONS: in historic Coloma, on the corner of Church and High Sts., around the corner from the museum and visitor's center.

Not only does the inn draw many wedding parties (couples can be married in the hilltop church and returned to the inn by horse-drawn carriage) but rafting groups and adventure-seekers, as well. Cindi's husband, Alan, is a commercial balloon pilot who will, by prior arrangement, take guests out for hot air and white-water balloon rides over the south fork of the American River. He launches the balloon from behind the inn, floats over the historic village of Coloma (where gold was first discovered), and can skim the basket right over the river rapids.

The living room.

The gracious interior suggests a genteel lifestyle.

MURPHY'S INN

Fresh sparkle and polish

Murphy's Inn was built in 1866 as an estate for a famous gold baron. One of the loveliest homes in town, it is also among the most pleasant inns in all of the Mother Lode country. The living room is filled with lovely antiques, and the lace curtains and floral wallpapers in the guest rooms gently evoke the past.

New owners Ted and Nancy Daus pride themselves not only on the atmosphere but on the facelift they have given the historic inn, reinvigorating it with a fresh sparkle and polish. From the big sunny breakfast room, guests can watch Nancy, a former caterer, whip up the morning repast: a garden quiche, coddled eggs, Belgian waffles, or a sausage casserole.

Visitors enjoy excellent cross-country and downhill skiing, swimming, jogging, and privileges at the Sierra Health Club. Just one block from town, they can browse through antiques shops, go to a movie, and dine in the Holbrooke Hotel and Pasta Luigi's.

A good innkeeper provides his guests with as many comforts as possible, whether it's keeping a fire blazing on the hearth or helping to plan a day of sightseeing, and Ted and Nancy do just that.

MURPHY'S INN, 318 Neal Street, Grass Valley, CA 95945; (800) 895-2488, (916) 273-6873; Ted and Nancy Daus, owners. Open all year. Eight rooms, including 3 suites, all with private baths and air conditioning. Rates: $95 to $140 per room, including full breakfast of Belgian waffles, garden quiche, or sausage casserole. Children welcome; no pets, smoking on deck only; Visa/MasterCard/American Express. The Holbrooke Hotel, Pasta Luigi, Pepper's recommended for dining. Gold panning, fishing, golf, boating in area; ski areas one hour away.

DIRECTIONS: from the south take Rte. 49 north to 174/Central Grass Valley exit. Turn left at first stop sign onto south Auburn and then left onto Neal Street at second stoplight. Go three blocks to corner of Neal and School Street.

Most of the bedrooms feature large armoires, handmade pine trunks containing bath towels, and American folk art. The luxurious master suite has a separate sitting room with an elaborately carved fireplace and a creamy couch. Upstairs, Mama and Papa's Room has a four-poster bed, navy blue wing-back chairs, and an extra-long bathtub. From Dawn's Room, you step down into a cheerful sun room that looks out over the garden. Gertie's Room has its own private entrance, kitchen, and a tub that is nearly as big as the grand white wicker bed.

Innkeeper Jeri Boka serves up a filling breakfast of savory delights such as Grandmere's eggs, a soufflé, a corn and chile casserole, a broccoli, mushroom, and cheese frittata, and homemade apple sauce and cookies.

GRANDMERE'S, 449 Broad St., Nevada City, CA 95959; (916) 265-4660; Jeri and Doug Boka, owners. Open all year, except for 4 days at Christmas. Seven rooms with private baths, including 1 suite with tub. Rates: $100 to $160 double, including full breakfast. Inquire about children; no pets; no smoking; Visa/MasterCard. Lively town abounds in things to do.

DIRECTIONS: from Sacramento on I-80 take Rte. 49 north at Auburn to Nevada City to Broad St. exit. Turn left on Broad for 3 blocks to inn.

GRANDMERE'S

A landmark for women's rights

Loaded with picturesque western-style buildings, unique shops, and cafés, Nevada City is one of the most appealing towns along the Gold Route. Just up Broad Street, atop Nabob Hill, Grandmere's, an 1856 inn, figured prominently in American history. Congressman Aaron Sargent, who wrote the ammendment giving women the right to vote, lived here, and Susan B. Anthony was a frequent guest.

The Colonial Revival exterior is painted cottage white, and all interior walls, carpets, and fresh bathroom tiles are cool grey and white. With its colorful country quilts and warm, overstuffed sofas, the house has a soothing effect. A veranda wraps around the front of the house; and in back, the garden slopes downhill, with benches for daydreaming.

Handmade quilts on all the beds.

THE RED CASTLE INN

A marvelous example of Gothic Revival

"The Castle," as locals once referred to it, stood out as a landmark of Nevada City when it was built in 1860. Perched high on Prospect Hill, it looked just like a gingerbread house with its four stories of red brick and white icicle wood trim. But now, 130 years later, the trees have grown so thick around the house, that it is almost totally hidden from sight.

Red Castle Inn is one of only two Gothic Revival brick buildings on the West Coast, and one of the first bed and breakfast inns in California. Mary Louise and Conley Weaver took over the inn five years ago and filled it with a vast collection of heirlooms (note the old-fashioned pump organ and telephone in the parlor, as well as the whimsical lamps) and original works of art, including two Bufano sculptures.

Seven bedrooms are dispersed over the four "cake layers," and each level has its own veranda or balcony. Rooms on the lower floor feature high ceilings, carved, canopied beds, French doors, and an eclectic array of floral curtain and wallpaper patterns. Still, many guests prefer the cozy top-most tier, likening it to being in a tree-house.

After a buffet breakfast of plums in port, müesli Ballymore, zucchini bread, apple pancakes, or perhaps crab and artichoke quiche, juice and a special blend of coffee, you can walk it off down the terraced, wooded path into town.

Many Victorian traditions, such as afternoon tea and classical music, patriotic summer bunting hung from the balconies, Saturday morning horse-drawn carriage rides through historic Nevada City, and a special sit-down Christmas dinner, are highlighted at the Red Castle Inn. In September, on Constitution Day, the whole town turns out for a fancy dress parade, fireworks, and Civil War re-enactment in nearby Pioneer Park.

THE RED CASTLE INN, 109 Prospect St., Nevada City, CA 95959; (916) 265-5135; Conley and Mary Louise Weaver, owners. Open all year. Seven rooms and suites, all with private baths. Rates: $95 to $140 per room, including full home-cooked breakfast. Children over 12 welcome; no pets; smoking on verandas only; Visa/MasterCard. Town's restaurants serve California, French, Continental cuisine. Many activities, including music festivals, theater arts.

DIRECTIONS: from south on I-80 take Rte. 49 north at Auburn to Sacramento St. exit at Nevada City. Pass Exxon station and turn right on Adams and left on Prospect.

The stunning Victorian Gothic inn building.

Lamp made from child's fitting form

DOWNEY HOUSE

An old-fashioned trendsetter

Just up the street from Grandmere's, Downey House is a newcomer with a different bent on the traditional bed and breakfast idea. Although the house is a gracious 1869 Victorian with elegant curving hallways and grooved wainscotting, the décor is decidedly muted Southwestern style. Downey House diverges from most other inns, too, in that its crisp, immaculate rooms are all quite similar.

Thick, off-white textured carpeting and cream-colored walls bring up the soft roses, lavender, purples, and greens of the bed linens. The subtle differences in each room stem primarily from these linens and from the bold paintings by Christine Johnson that mirror the colors and feelings of the sheet designs. Built-in beds rely on a creative alternative to standard headboards: a backdrop of faux rose-colored marble flanked by faux columns. The effect is stunning and restful, appealing to both men and women.

The gem of Downey House, however, is innkeeper Miriam Wright. Miriam claims, "I want to be a trendsetter," but she's one of the best old-fashioned hostesses to be found anywhere. She makes fresh-ground coffee and fresh-squeezed juice in the morning to go with amazingly good home-baked sweet breads, yeast rolls, and crustless quiche or custard omelet. "I buy the fruits from local farmers; they're organic, fresh, and sweet," says Miriam, who also chooses the Hooper chocolates that await the guests in their rooms.

Host Miriam Wright sets the impeccable style at Downey House.

DOWNEY HOUSE, 517 W. Broad Street, Nevada City, CA 95959; (916) 265-2815; Miriam Wright, innkeeper. Six rooms, all with private bath. Rates: $75 to $100. Includes full buffet breakfast, access to stocked refrigerator with soft drinks, and a never-empty cookie jar. Complimentary wine at 5 o'clock. No smoking inside; no pets; MasterCard/Visa accepted. Brewery, mine tour, bicycle rental, swimming, hiking, fishing, tennis, golf, horseback riding, and cross-country skiing nearby.

DIRECTIONS: from the south, take Rte. 49 to the Broad St. exit. Take a left onto Broad and go through town to the top of the hill. The house is on the left, on the corner of Broad and Bennett. From the north, take the Broad St. exit off Hwy. 49 and take a right onto Broad St., then follow the directions above.

The lobby.

TRUCKEE HOTEL

Hotel living as it used to be

Originally built as a stage stop in the late 1860s, The Truckee Hotel was also home to transcontinental railroad laborers, lumber mill workers, and ice harvesters before it welcomed tourists at the turn of the century. During its 1991 restoration, the four-story hotel was given a facelift, but its historic quirks, such as the uneven floors and door frames, were left intact.

On the main level is a new-looking, Victorian-style parlor with marble fireplace where a continental buffet breakfast is served each morning. The second-level guest rooms are the most comfortable, with private baths and claw foot tubs. On the third and fourth floors, the European-style rooms have sinks in the rooms and shared baths. All thirty-four rooms are decorated in light Victorian schemes, with soft print wallpaper, bedspreads, and antique carved or iron beds. Room 122 is particularly pretty, with a four-poster canopy bed, cream and gold-tinged spread, velvet chairs, and angel prints here and

THE TRUCKEE HOTEL, 10007 Bridge St., PO Box 884, Truckee, CA 96160; (800) 659-6921; (916) 587-4444; Fax (916) 587-1599; Jeff & Karen Winter, owners; Rachelle L. Pellissier, manager. Open all year. Eight suites with private baths and twenty-eight rooms with shared baths. Rates: $60 to $115, including expanded continental breakfast. Children welcome; no smoking; Spanish spoken; no pets; Visa/MasterCard/American Express. Ski lockers provided at the hotel. Conference room on premises. Hiking, biking, swimming, skiing, and boating also nearby. The Passage recommended for dining.

DIRECTIONS: from I-80, exit at Central Truckee. Proceed east on Donner Pass Rd. for two blocks.

there. There are no phones, televisions or clocks in any of the guest quarters.

Truckee is a small town north of Lake Tahoe in the Sierra Nevada Mountains. Within a twenty-mile radius are a dozen ski resorts. The hotel is centrally located on a short, bustling main street of gift shops, lively bars, and restaurants. Also nearby is the railroad depot, which can be rather noisy at times. In case the sound of passing trains keeps you awake at night, the hotel provides ear plugs in every guest room.

Room 122.

WINE COUNTRY

CHURCHILL MANOR

Romance with a capital R

Churchill Manor has a ninety-year history of weddings, and it's easy to see why. The pink-and-white-trimmed 1889 mansion is surrounded by stately white columns, a wide veranda, and expansive lawn with over fifty varieties of gorgeous roses. The spacious front parlor is highlighted by Oriental carpets atop wood floors, leather sofas, redwood paneling, beveled leaded glass, and burgundy velvet curtains. Adjoining this is the Music Room, an exquisite salon with chandelier and grand piano. The common rooms lead further to a dining room, game room, and sun room where the floors are laid with over sixty thousand original tiles. Altogether, there's plenty of elbow room—ten thousand square feet, to be exact.

Today, nearly fifty weddings a year are still per-formed at the inn, thanks to the tireless efforts of innkeepers Joanna Guidotti and Brian Jensen. In addition to running the inn and raising their young son, they do all the planning and catering for every wedding. Brian also cooks breakfast for the guests, and Joanna says, "His omelets are to die for."

On the second and third floors are ten pretty guest rooms, each filled with romantic antiques, original furnishings, and fixtures. Rose's Room, for instance, has twenty-four-carat gold trim on its white fireplace tiles, with a big tub standing on claw feet nearby.

Despite its elegance, the inn isn't a look-but-don't-touch kind of place. Brian and Joanna are an informal couple who make their guests feel at ease.

CHURCHILL MANOR, 485 Brown St., Napa, CA 94559; (707) 253-7733; Fax (707) 253-8836; Brian Jensen & Joanna Guidotti, owners. Open all year. Ten rooms, all with private baths. Rates: $75 to $145, including full breakfast, afternoon cookies, and evening wine and cheese. Children under 12 allowed if a group reserves all 10 rooms; smoking permitted outside only; some Spanish spoken; no pets; all credit cards accepted. Complimentary tandem bicycles and croquet available. Wineries, balloon rides, Napa Valley Wine Train, and downtown Napa nearby. French Laundry, Chanterelle, and Don Giovanni's recommended for dining.

DIRECTIONS: from Hwy. 29, exit at First St./Central Napa. Follow "downtown Napa" signs onto Second St. Turn right on Jefferson St., left on Oak St., and proceed 7 blocks to corner of Oak and Brown Sts.

Left above, Joanna Guidotti and Brian Jensen with son Adam and Ziggy the dog. Below, the front parlor and music room.

Rose's Room.

OLD WORLD INN

Homemade truffles

Built in 1900 by a local contractor as a private town residence, The Old World Inn combines an eclectic mix of architectural styles with details such as wood shingles, clinker brick, bevelled and leaded glass, and wide, shady porches.

The interior of the inn is a pastel wonderland of draped fabrics, pleats, ruffles, and bows inspired by the soft colors of Swedish artist Carl Larsson. Everything is coordinated to a designer's fantasy. The Victorian furnishings are painted soft blue, apricot, mint green, or pink to match each room. In the living room chintz-covered love seats arranged on a pastel Dhurrie carpet, a mantel covered with Pooh bears and quilted hearts, and immense bows stenciled above the moldings—together create an air of romance and whimsy.

There is a generous assortment of food. Beginning at breakfast, there are muffins, croissants, nut breads, and coffee cakes. A main entrée of crêpes or frittatas is beautifully accompanied by an arrangement of decoratively sliced fruits.

Tea time is an event. Scottish shortbread, sugar and spice cookies, and chocolate cake are but a few of the homemade treats. At wine tasting hour around 5:30 or 6 P.M., gourmet cheeses are presented with French bread, garlic toast, and savory patés.

But it is at dessert time that the Old World Inn really excels. After an evening out, didn't we always come home and raid the fridge? Bite-sized mocha cookies, chocolate walnut fudge, and amaretto torte too good to believe, chocolate box cake made of crushed cookies, pistachios, and grand marnier, and rum truffles all provide that "little something" to satisfy a late night sweet tooth.

OLD WORLD INN, 1301 Jefferson Street, Napa, CA 94559; (707) 257-0112; Diane Dumaine, owner. Eight rooms, each with private bath. Rates: $110 to $145. Two-night minimum on Sat. night stays. Includes an abundance of foods from morning to just before midnight! Custom built Jacuzzi. No children; no pets; no smoking in the house; Visa/MasterCard/American Express.

DIRECTIONS: from San Francisco via Golden Gate Bridge: north on US-101 to exit 37; follow to Rte. 121 and then left onto Rte. 29. Take Lincoln East exit, proceed 1/2 mile, and make a right onto Jefferson.

The Carl Larsson Room is the consummate bridal suite.

JOSEPH WOODS PHOTOGRAPH

LA RESIDENCE

For lovers of haute cuisine

Owned and operated by innkeepers David Jackson and Craig Claussen, La Résidence offers Napa Valley guests the best of both worlds—stylish yet casual accommodations.

Built in 1870 by a prosperous sheep and cattle rancher, the mansion boasts Greek Revival detailing and a Victorian addition appended to the building at the turn of the century. Cabernet Hall, a vast French Provincial-style barn, is the other half of the inn complex, joined to the mansion by a beautifully landscaped garden complete with flower beds, grape arbors, a gazebo, and a swimming pool.

The center of activity is Cabernet Hall, where a red-brick floor leads to the breakfast room and to a staircase ascending to the spacious guest rooms. Furnished in a harmonious blend of Laura Ashley and Pierre Deux fabrics, the rooms offer a pleasing mix of antique oak and unfinished pieces. Each room has a working fireplace, and French doors facing onto the barn's wraparound porches.

Breakfast consists of a fresh fruit course followed by an egg dish or quiche. Freshly baked pastries and breads, teas, and a special blended coffee round out the breakfast fare. The evening aperitif hour allows guests to sample the inn's fine selection of Napa wines.

LA RÉSIDENCE, 4066 St. Helena Highway N., Napa, CA 94558; (707) 253-0337, Fax (707) 253-0382; David R. Jackson and Craig E. Claussen, owners. Twenty rooms total, most with private baths, most with fireplaces; 9 are in the "Mansion"; 11 are in the "French Barn," with balconies and patios. Rates: $100 to $235. Includes full breakfast and wine Social in the afternoon. Children accepted; no pets; Spa/Jacuzzi; heated swimming pool; Visa/MasterCard/American Express/ Diners Club.

DIRECTIONS: from San Francisco, US-101 to Rte. 37 to Rte. 12. Proceed onto Rte. 29 to North Napa and first right turn after Salvador Ave.

Gothic Revival built by a New Orleans river pilot.

VILLA ST. HELENA

Rooms with vineyard views

Villa St. Helena is an expansive Mediterranean-style villa hidden in the hills of the Mayacamas Mountains above St. Helena. Located 65 miles north of San Francisco, this secluded twenty-acre estate combines architectural virtuosity with panoramic views of scenic Napa Valley and its vineyards.

The scale of the Villa is impressive at twelve thousand square feet, and yet the symmetry and simplicity of its architecture encourages informality. The wood-paneled library is cozy and comforting should one want to quietly peruse the extensive collection of wine-related books and magazines. In contrast, the living room is very grand and festive with warmth generated by sun pouring in from the solarium or from a fire burning in the huge stone hearth.

Hundreds of cymbidium orchids flourish in the courtyard, solarium, and on the verandas under the watchful eye of owners Ralph and Carolyn Cotton. Sharing their villa is a joy, as there is a particular elegance to the palatial home and splendid grounds. The expansive grassy courtyard lures guests to step out from glass-enclosed verandas and enjoy lounging by or swimming in the Villa's spacious pool. The backdrop for the pool and its adjacent patio and brick barbeque is an eliptical arched red brick wall carved into the hillside, creating a harmonious blend of natural beauty and masterful design. So fabulous is the setting that this courtyard was chosen for the shooting of a few party scenes for *Falconcrest*.

VILLA ST. HELENA, 2727 Sulphur Springs Avenue, St. Helena, CA 94574; (707) 963-2514; Ralph & Carolyn Cotton, owners. Three suites, each with private bath and spacious quarters. Rates: $165 to $245. Includes a bountiful and delicious breakfast served in solarium, with a selection of cheeses and bread and a variety of baked or fresh fruits and mixed fruit juices. Complimentary bottle of wine each evening. No children; no pets; Visa/MasterCard/American Express. Tilly is the cat in residence.

DIRECTIONS: from Rte. 29 take a left onto Sulphur Springs Ave. Proceed approximately 1½ miles and look for a sign on mail boxes on the left. Take a left, go through a gate, and follow the private driveway ¾ of a mile to top of hill.

COUNTRY MEADOW INN

Where time slows down

Susan Hardesty brings to the job of innkeeping all of her loves: cooking, decorating, Victoriana, visiting with people, and living in the country. Guests at the Country Meadow Inn immediately sense that when they visit the farmhouse, set on six acres of rolling meadows in California's fabled wine country.

There is much relaxing to do here—in the solar heated pool and on the newly installed tennis court.

The picnic bench under the oak beckons, as do the decks at the pool and the house.

Flower gardens abound. There are rose bushes, iris, and poppies, and there are vegetable gardens and berry bushes bearing strawberries and blackberries that are made into jams.

Breakfast, a three-course affair, is served around the dining room table. Green chile quiche, oatmeal pancakes, eggs, fruit salad, muffins, and coffee cake are some of the offerings. And there are pitchers of lemonade, crackers, and herbed cheese for afternoon refreshment.

Furnished in Victorian style, the rooms are romantic and inviting. The atmosphere is friendly and the innkeeper makes you feel right at home.

COUNTRY MEADOW INN. 11360 Old Redwood Hwy., Windsor, CA 95492; (707) 431-1276, (800) 238-1728; Susan Hardesty, owner. Open all year. Five period guest rooms, including one luxury suite, all with private baths. Rates: $95 to $165 per room, including full gourmet country breakfast. Children over 12 welcome; no pets; smoking outside only; Visa/MasterCard. Wonderful restaurants 5 minutes away. Swimming, fishing, canoeing on the Russian River; antiques shops and wine tasting at over 100 local wineries.

DIRECTIONS: from US-101 north take Healdsburg Ave. exit. Turn left on Old Redwood Hwy. for 2 miles to inn, which is 200 yards past Piper Sonoma Cellars and Rodney Strong Wineries. From 101 south take Old Redwood Hwy. exit and turn right.

The Mahogany Room.

Gorgeous antiques.

MAISON FLEURIE

The Four Sisters come to Yountville

Maison Fleurie, formerly the Magnolia Hotel, in Yountville, is one of the newest additions to the Four Sisters Inns. The three turn-of-the-century buildings have been spruced up and given a French country look along with a friendly staff, amenities, and teddy bears for which the Four Sisters Inns are so well known.

All three buildings are built of brick and covered with ivy. The main building, which was once a bordello, is most atmospheric, with thick stone walls, terra cotta tiled floors, and deep-set windows. Most of these seven rooms overlook a vineyard across the way. Four more luxurious bedrooms with fireplaces (and some with Jacuzzi tubs) are found in the former bakery (once ironically called the Four Sisters Bakery). Two other rooms are in a carriage house next

Left, the lush garden and inn building.

to the swimming pool and spa. The garden and courtyards tie the guest quarters gracefully together.

A full breakfast is served in one of the two parlors before a crackling fireplace. Guests can also enjoy an afternoon tea of wine and hors d'oeuvres. And if you're still hungry during the day, there are home-baked cookies in a bottomless jar on the mantel.

Yountville is a town that begs to be explored, full of shops, wineries, and wonderful restaurants. Domaine Chandon, one of the country's finest makers of sparkling wines, offers fascinating tours and a fabulous restaurant. It's just a short ride away, and the inn provides complimentary mountain bikes with that very thought in mind.

MAISON FLEURIE, 6529 Yount St., Yountville, CA 94599; (800) 788-0369; (707) 944-2056; Fax (707) 944-9342; Roger Asbill, manager. Open all year. Thirteen rooms in three buildings, all with private baths. Rates: $110 to $190, including hearty country breakfast and afternoon wine and hors d'oeuvres. Children welcome; no smoking; no pets; all credit cards accepted. Swimming pool and spa on premises. Mountain bikes available. Domaine Chandon, Chardonnay Golf Course, Napa Valley Wine Train, and ballooning nearby.

DIRECTIONS: from Hwy. 29, exit at Yountville. Turn right, then left on Washington St. At the fork, stay to the right on Yount St.

Some of the superb carpenters' gothic gables that make the house so distinctive.

THE GABLES INN

A Gothic Revival farmhouse

This Victorian Gothic Revival house is on the National Historic Register, and remains largely unchanged since its 19th-century dairy-farming days. The old gray barn still has names of its former bovine inhabitants such as "Bessy," "Emma," and "Spot" written above each stall. An antique outhouse sits by the seasonal creek. Inside the fifteen-gabled house are three original, Italian-marble fireplaces that were brought around Cape Horn. A mahogany staircase spirals gracefully upward to the five guest rooms.

Zilpha Keatley Snyder wrote many of her famous children's books here, while raising her family from the 1960s–80s. Some of her stories, such as *The Headless Cupid*, are easily imagined as taking place at The Gables.

Michael and Judy Ogne, the present owners, fell in love with the idea of innkeeping when they first stayed at an inn years ago. They, along with their two teen-aged daughters, are enthusiastically grow-

ing vegetables, raising chickens, and taking good care of their guests. Their full country-gourmet breakfasts include zucchini and sausage frittatas or French toast with Grand Marnier sauce, and cocoa/spice muffins. After a day of winery or antique-shopping, guests can return to the tranquil sun deck for afternoon refreshments.

The bedrooms are all spacious with high, angular ceilings, lots of light, and keyhole-shaped windows. The upstairs rooms all have claw-footed tubs. Out back is a separate honeymoon cottage called William and Mary.

The Gables Inn is perfect for those looking for both a rural escape and proximity to the wineries of the Sonoma Valley. In summertime, the three-and-a-half acres of golden fields are scented with rosemary, and in springtime, vivid yellow mustard flowers bloom.

THE GABLES INN, 4257 Petaluma Hill Road, Santa Rosa, CA 95404; (707) 585-7777; Michael and Judy Ogne, owners. Open all year. Seven guest rooms in main house, 1 in cottage, all with private baths. Rates: $95 to $145 per room; cottage $135. Includes full country gourmet breakfast. Children over 10 preferred; no pets; no smoking; Visa/MasterCard/American Express/Discover. Recommended restaurants include La Gare, Lisa Hemenways, Matisse, John Ash. In the Russian River resort area—75 premium wineries to visit.

DIRECTIONS: from US-101 north exit onto Rohnert Park Expressway east for 2½ miles to Petaluma Hill Road and go north for 4 miles to inn.

The elegant foyer staircase.

LOCAL COLOR PHOTOGRAPH

BRANNON COTTAGE

An experienced innkeeper

Listed on the National Register of Historic Places, this Greek Revival Victorian inn was built by Sam Brannan, co-founder of the cities of San Francisco and Sacramento. Designed as a guest house for the original spa, all six of its stenciled and lace-curtained rooms have private entrances that open onto lovely gardens, and names like Iris, Poppy, and Wild Rose. A cozy lounge and a dining room with a fireplace serve as a backdrop for the display of fine art and antiques.

An experienced innkeeper, Peter Bach, the charming host, is the resident gardener, plumber, and chef. Mornings find him serving up a buffet breakfast that includes a casserole of spinach and eggs, ham and eggs, or a vegetable omelet. Weather permitting, guests enjoy breakfast in the garden along with the morning paper.

The inn is only minutes from some of California's most famous wineries and champagne houses. Biking, gliding, horseback riding, and hot air ballooning are all within easy access. Fine restaurants abound and there are public tennis courts and a spa pool within sight. You can walk to your favorite spa for a mudbath or massage.

Mr. Bach can arrange spa times, winery visits, and make reservations for special intimate dinners in some hidden nook or gourmet eatery.

BRANNAN COTTAGE INN, 100 Wapoo Avenue, Calistoga, CA 94515; (707) 942-4200; Peter Bach, owner. Six rooms, all with private baths and private entrances. Rates: $110 to $160, with special rates in mid-week off season, November to March. Includes full breakfast. No children under 12; no smoking; no pets; Visa/MasterCard. Handicap Access.

DIRECTIONS: north on Rte. 29 to Calistoga. Right on Lincoln Avenue (main street) past Glider Airport. Left onto Wapoo.

CAMELLIA INN

Simple grace and elegance

Built in 1869, the Camellia Inn is an early example of an Italianate Victorian building whose lines are exceptionally simple and graceful. Keeping the Victorian furnishings to a refreshing minimum allows the architecture to speak for itself. High ceilings, twin white marble fireplaces in two adjacent parlors, and tall, arched windows are all enhanced by natural light reflected off the salmon colored walls. Silk-screened wallpaper, a hand-crocheted bedspread, and satin pillows add just the right touches in the guest rooms.

Two of the rooms, Moon Glow and Demitasse, are in the main house and share a classic 1920s green-tiled bathroom. Moon Glow is named for the soft moonlight that shines through the cedar trees into the spacious room. Demitasse, overlooking an outdoor fishpond, is named for its coziness and charm. The remaining four rooms, located in a separate building, are reached by

The quiet elegance of the entrance hall.

crossing a breezeway. A favorite room, once the original dining room of the home, and now called the Royalty Suite, has a massive maple tester bed brought from a castle in Scotland.

Camellia Inn is a wonderful place to visit in any season. On chilly mornings a fire in the breakfast room adds romance as well as warmth. In summer, you can sip a glass of wine under the shade trees near the large swimming pool.

A stay at the Camellia Inn often includes a tour of owners' Ray and Del Lewand's home-style wine-making facilities.

CAMELLIA INN, 211 North Street, Healdsburg, CA 95448; (707) 433-8182, (800) 727-8182, Fax (707) 433-8130; Ray and Del Lewand, owners. Nine rooms, seven with private baths, several with private entrances. Each furnished with period antiques. Rates: $70 to $135. Includes full breakfast of fresh fruit, homemade breads, and eggs. Guests are invited to join the hosts for refreshments in the evening. Children welcome; no pets; smoking in designated areas; Visa/MasterCard/American Express. Swimming pool. Two blocks from town square. Over 40 wineries within seven miles and good fishing for steelhead not far away.

DIRECTIONS: from US-101 take the second Healdsburg exit. Proceed north for three blocks and turn right onto North Street.

Gigantic antique beds dominate the sun-filled guest rooms.

MADRONA MANOR

A gourmet's bed and breakfast on an eight-acre garden estate

Built as a vacation retreat for a wealthy San Francisco businessman in 1881, expense appears to have been of no concern here. The ceilings are high, and the several parlors off the hallway are large and elegant. A broad staircase leads to four spacious master suites, each of which either has a large bay window or opens out onto a balcony.

Many of the furnishings in both the Manor and adjacent Carriage House are original to the estate and are important examples of American Victorian Renaissance style. There is an elegant mahogany four-poster bed dating from the mid-1800s and a full suite of matching carved walnut and burled wood dressers and headboard. The music room of the Manor remains the same, with the original rosewood square grand piano still in place.

Part of the eight-acre estate is planted with luxurious flower gardens and a citrus grove. Foxgloves, delphiniums, tulips, irises, daffodils, sweet peas, and zinnias find their way into the rooms. "People from the east who have never picked an orange go out and do it and think it's just wonderful," laughs owner Carol Muir.

What was at one time the billiard room is now one of the two dining rooms of Madrona Manor, where gourmet meals are served to guests and to the public. The cuisine is orchestrated by several chefs who use a brick oven, smokehouse, orchard, and vegetable-herb garden to provide memorable meals. Having a restaurant in-house adds an unexpected luxury to this grand bed and breakfast estate.

MADRONA MANOR, 1001 Westside Road, Box 818, Healdsburg, CA 95448; (707) 433-4231, (800) 258-4003, Fax (707) 433-0703; Carol and John Muir, owners; Todd Muir, executive chef, Richard Puma, pastry chef. Geno Ceccato, resident landscape architect, and Mark Muir, resident maintenance manager. Twenty-one rooms, some with fireplaces, all with private baths; nine in manor and balance in carriage house and adjacent buildings. Rates: low and high season range from $140 to $240, including full breakfast in dining room or on outdoor terrace. Children welcome; manageable pets by arrangement; smoking allowed on grounds; all credit cards accepted. Wheelchair access to one downstairs bedroom. Swimming pool.

DIRECTIONS: from US-101, take the second Healdsburg exit. At the first stoplight, make a left onto Mill Street. In approximately ¾ of a mile the road turns to the left and the arched white gateway to the major is straight ahead.

A Typical guest cottage.

The 1925 Star tourer.

PHOTOGRAPHS COURTESY BELLE DE JOUR

BELLE DE JOUR INN

A sophisticated, intimate retreat

The approach to Belle de Jour, up a tree-lined, sloping driveway, hints at the understated elegance to come. Custis Piper, a direct descendant of Martha Custis Washington, turned the 1873 house and its cottages into a bed and breakfast in 1975, but Tom and Brenda Hearn worked the magic that transformed it into an intimate, sophisticated retreat.

The Hearns, in separate cars both equipped with telephones, stuck in the normal Los Angeles freeway traffic, decided they'd "had it with L.A." Brenda left a career as a troubleshooter for IBM; Tom, as a manufacturer's representative for consumer electronics. Now they revel in their six acres that many guests compare to central Italy or the Loire Valley.

It's not unusual to see Tom mowing the lawn, then dipping into the "cool pool"—a 25,000-gallon wine vat cut down to twelve feet across and four feet deep. Another outdoor diversion, the hammock under a big oak, draws even the most active guests into heavenly indolence; it's so easy to relax here.

Each of the four cottage bedrooms incorporates outdoor space for private cloud-watching or star-gazing. Occasionally Tom will take out his catadioptric telescope for more serious astral observation.

"Our social hour," however, "is at breakfast," says Tom. "We help people plan their day." Choosing a winery itinerary, plotting bicycle routes, or signing up for a picnic ride in the Hearns' 1925 Star over a morning meal of heart-shaped waffles with orange sauce starts the day with near-perfection.

BELLE DE JOUR INN, 16276 Healdsburg Avenue, Healdsburg, CA 95448; (707) 433-7892; Tom and Brenda Hearn, owners. Four cottage rooms with private baths, all with woodstove or fireplace and three with whirlpool baths. Rates: $125 to $185. Includes full breakfast. No smoking; no pets; three cats live on the property including Ivan the Terrible; MasterCard/Visa/Discover. Dipping pool, hammocks, picnic table on premises; old car tours to wineries by arrangement. Bicycle rental, tennis, golf, canoe rental, sailing nearby. Good restaurants and many wineries in the immediate area.

DIRECTIONS: take US-101 to the Dry Creek Rd. exit and go east to Healdsburg Ave. Turn left at the lights and go north for approximately 1 mile. The inn's driveway is located directly across from the Simi Winery.

The Caretaker's Suite boasts a Shaker-style pencil post bed and a Franklin wood stove.

HOPE-BOSWORTH
HOPE-MERRILL

Two homes restored in style

Careful research and painstaking attention to detail by innkeeper Rosalie Hope are evident throughout Hope-Merrill and Hope-Bosworth homes. The houses, across from each other on Geyserville's main street, reflect different periods and therefore differing styles and moods.

The Hope-Bosworth House.

Hope-Merrill, built around the 1880s, is an Eastlake and Stick Victorian with formal lines. The interior is similar in design, with elegant wainscoting, a carved banister on a curved stairway, and high graceful windows. The home has been awarded accolades for its authentic décor, which includes lovely period antiques, a Victorian dollhouse, a fire screen embroidered with calla lilies, Parrish lithographs, and bountiful displays of Victorian memorabilia, including a glass case of beaded handbags.

Hope-Bosworth, built in 1904, is a "pattern-book house," built from plans selected and ordered from catalogs offering the popular contemporary styles of the day. It is predictably simpler in design and mood. The building is more square, and the rooms are symmetrical; the staircase climbs at utilitarian right angles. With pale oak and wicker furnishings and patterned wallpapers, the overall décor is less ceremonious, giving a country feeling to the house.

HOPE-BOSWORTH AND HOPE-MERRILL, 21238 Geyserville Ave., Geyserville, CA 95441; (707) 857-3356, (800) 825-4233, Fax (707) 857-4073; Rosalie Hope, owner. Four rooms in one house, eight in the other. Private baths, 3 with Jacuzzi tubs. Rates: $95 to $140. Includes a gourmet breakfast. No pets; no smoking; Visa/MasterCard/American Express. Heated pool and Victorian gardens. Special wine tours conducted from the premises, including picnic lunch baskets (by advance reservation).

DIRECTIONS: from US-101, exit at Geyserville; the houses are across the street from one another on the main street of Geyserville.

Above, the ornate bed dominates this guest room.

APPLEWOOD

Serene and elegant

Serene and elegant, Applewood is a far cry from the usual rustic vacation cabins found around Guerneville. Its white stucco walls, tiled roof, and beamed ceilings give the inn a graceful Spanish appearance. The home was designed in the Mission Revival-style by renowned architect Carl Warnecke in 1922. During the 1980s, the estate, which included six acres of redwoods, was purchased by Darryl Notter and Jim Caron, who refurbished the home at great expense, and converted it to an inn.

In 1995, another building was completed with an additional seven rooms, each with its own fireplace, some with a shower-for-two, and featuring a luxurious penthouse suite with cathedral ceiling and private sundeck that covers the entire third floor.

Finely-made furniture and original artwork are hallmarks of the inn, complemented by deluxe mattresses, imported feather comforters, cut crystal water glasses, and fresh roses.

Left, an attractive part of the lounge is flooded with California sunshine by the skylights.

Gourmet breakfasts of French toast marinated in Grand Marnier and peaches, or eggs Florentine can be savored for breakfast. And elegant dinners are available Tuesday through Saturday.

APPLEWOOD INN, (*formerly The Estate Inn*) 13555 Hwy. 116, Guerneville, CA 95446; (707) 869-9093; James J. Caron and Darryl Notter, owners. Open all year. Sixteen rooms in two buildings with private baths and queen beds. Rates: $125 to $250 per room, including full breakfast. Prix fixe dinner optional Tuesday through Sat. Children not permitted because of liquor license; no pets; no smoking; Visa/MasterCard/American Express/Discover. Horseback riding, canoeing, tennis, golf, winery tours, Japanese enzyme baths.

DIRECTIONS: from US-101 north go through Santa Rosa and take River Road/Guerneville exit and go 14 miles west to Guerneville. At first stop sign turn left onto Rte. 116 and cross Russian River bridge and go ½ mile to inn.

The living room.

INN AT OCCIDENTAL

An inveterate collector

The Inn at Occidental is a superior B&B not least of all because of its personable innkeeper, Jack Bullard. Always on hand to welcome new guests, he makes a real effort to give everyone special attention. A former Bostonian and law executive, Jack took over and remodeled the Inn at Occidental two years ago.

His eight-room Victorian is tastefully appointed. In the living room, navy blue sofas and traditional American antiques are ornamented by Jack's collection of clocks, fine books, silver, flower, and orchid arrangements. Many of the bedrooms feature fresh white Battenburg comforters over featherbeds, with bold patchwork quilts folded at the foot of each bed. On the walls, in place of the usual flowery pictures, are striking black and white nature photographs, many taken by Jack. His collection of antique glass, silver and pottery are generously scattered throughout the rooms.

Left above, the Cut Glass Room.
showing some of the photographs over the bed.

Breakfast, which can be eaten in the dining room or on the wicker-filled sunporch, includes local blueberries and strawberries, yogurt, homemade granola, freshly-baked croissants, and a hot entrée. Among Jack's specialties are apple-thyme pancakes with Vermont maple or homemade orange syrup, vegetable quiche, and croissant French toast.

Just a stroll down the hill is the little town of Occidental, known for over a century as the "home of family-style dinners." The aroma of marinara sauce emanates from the town square, where numerous Italian family-style restaurants still thrive.

INN AT OCCIDENTAL, 3657 Church St., Occidental, CA 95465; (800) 522-6324; (707) 874-1047; Fax (707) 874-1078; Jack Bullard, owner/innkeeper. Open all year. Six rooms and two suites (one designed for the physically challenged), all with private baths. Rates: $95 to $195, including full breakfast. Children over 10 welcome; smoking allowed outside; some French and Spanish spoken; no pets; all credit cards accepted. Corporate meetings (conference room available) and weddings can be arranged. Russian River activities, Sonoma Coast beaches, wineries, horseback riding, Osmosis Enzyme Bath and Massage, specialty nurseries and gardens nearby. Willowside Cafe, Union Hotel, and Bohemian Cafe recommended for dining.

DIRECTIONS: from SR-116 west in downtown Sebastopol, take SR-12 toward Bodega Bay. Proceed about 6.5 miles and turn right on the Bohemian Hwy. to Occidental. Turn right at Occidental's downtown stop sign and head up the hill to the inn.

NORTHERN CALIFORNIA

THE PELICAN INN

Shakespeare could have slept here

Perfectly natural in its wooded seaside park setting, this sixteenth-century-style English country manor exudes the hospitality and comfort of the old English pub and inn. There is a full complement of English beers on tap, a fire blazes on the full hearth, and folks are gathered with mugs of ale or cups of mulled wine cheering players at the dart board. For lunch, cottage pies and bangers and mash are served on long, candlelit wooden tables which are also used in the evening for serving prime rib and beef Wellington. And as the English might say, "there is good fellowship in plentiful proportions."

Upstairs are seven rooms, all continuing the sixteenth-century theme. Canopied beds, lovely antiques, and recessed leaded windows enhance the feeling of taking a step back in time. There is even a step stool to help you get into the high old bed. Fresh cut flowers and complimentary Harvey's Bristol Cream add welcoming touches.

Never has a 400-year-old inn, restaurant, and pub been so authentically replicated. It is the realization of one man's dream, Charles Felix, who wanted to resurrect an English west country family inn, following the tradition of his preceding five generations of publicans. Built in 1979, and twenty minutes from San Francisco, the Pelican is indeed in another world. The fascination and appeal of the Pelican are perhaps best reflected by the need to reserve a weekend six months in advance.

THE PELICAN INN, Muir Beach, CA 94965; (415) 383-6000; Barry (a Devonshire man), publican. Seven rooms, each with private bath. Queen-size beds and half testers in each very English room. Rates: $143 to $165. Includes a hearty English breakfast of juice, toast, bacon, eggs, bangers (English pork sausages), fruit, and broiled tomatoes. Breakfast in bed available. Children welcome and rollaway beds, cribs are available; no pets; Visa/MasterCard.

DIRECTIONS: twenty minutes from Golden Gate Bridge on Hwy 1. From US-101, take Stinson Beach/Highway 1 exit and stay to the left on Hwy 1. Inn is 5 miles from traffic lights at Arco gas station.

BLACKTHORNE INN

A magical place

The Blackthorne is a product of the late sixties and early seventies, when people were building adventurous, nonconformist dream houses. Located in a canyon near Point Reyes National Seashore, it is a stunning example of an imaginative person's nontraditional approaches to living space. The Blackthorne, in fact, looks like an elegant treehouse.

Endlessly fascinating with its multiple levels, the Blackthorne is a series of interconnecting decks, handcrafted details, stained-glass windows, skylights—and a firepole for the limber to get from one level to another. There is a large stone hearth, laid by the Blackthorne's owner.

A four-story spiral staircase leads to an octagonal room in the building's tower. Known as the Eagle's Nest, the room has windows on every side and can also be reached by a forty-foot catwalk that connects with the highest of four decks. A thick blue carpet and Japanese futon are the only furnishings, making the treetops and sky the true decorative elements.

Perfect for the young at heart, the Blackthorne is one of the most romantic of the bed and breakfasts. There is every convenience here, including modern shared bathrooms, full hearty breakfasts, and the opportunity to try side-by-side tubs on a redwood deck. The Blackthorne is magical.

BLACKTHORNE INN 266 Vallejo Ave., P.O. Box 712, Inverness, CA 94937; (415) 663-8621, Fax (415) 663-8635; Bill and Susan Wigert, owners. Five rooms with private and shared baths. Rates: $105 to $195. Includes expanded continental breakfast of fruits, cereals, yogurt, breads, quiche, and coffee cakes. Children 14 and over; no pets; Visa/MasterCard. Pt. Reyes National Seashore nearby with miles of hiking trails and beautiful seashore.

DIRECTIONS: take US-101 to Sir Francis Drake Blvd. exit and proceed west to Olema. Take a right turn onto Rte. 1. Proceed about two miles and make a left turn towards Inverness. Go 1 mile and take a left onto Vallejo just before Perry's Inverness Park Grocery.

The original main inn.

The ocean beach across the road from the inn.

ST. ORRES

Twenty years of fun and success

Pine Haven, one of the new cottages.

The copper onion domes of St. Orres serve as fanciful reminders of the former Russian inhabitants who settled in Bodega Bay during the 1800s to establish their fur trade. Set across from a magnificent stretch of Northern California coastline, St. Orres resembles an elaborate, nineteenth-century dacha, or country house. Actually, it was handcrafted in 1977 out of weathered, century-old redwood and stained-glass windows. Over the years, various cottages—some looking like miniatures of the inn—were added to the pine-covered slope. Comfortably separated, each of the eleven cottages have a different personality, and some perennial guests have tried them all. The cottages are usually favored over the small upstairs bedrooms in the main lodge, which share 'his,' 'her,' and 'ours' baths.

Today, nearly twenty years later, the original owners—designer-builder Eric Black, manager Ted Black and chef Rosemary Campiformio—are still hands-on innkeepers at St. Orres. Rosemary is the creative hand behind the inn's renowned, award-winning restaurant. Her North Coast cuisine (with an emphasis on wild game and produce) is divinely flavored and cleverly presented. A typical dinner,

Left, the much photographed famous tower that houses the dining room.

enjoyed in the striking, three-story domed dining room, might begin with fresh-baked rosemary bread and cold cucumber-raisin-walnut soup. A light interlude of mixed greens and jicama stars is followed by a seafood surprise—baby steelhead salmon with Dungeness crab, spinach, and wild mushrooms—wrapped like a birthday present in parchment paper and ribbons. Their desserts are not to be missed.

ST. ORRES, 36601 Hwy. 1, PO Box 523, Gualala, CA 95445; (707) 884-3335; Fax (707) 884-1543; Rosemary Campiformio, Eric Black, and Charles T. Black, owners. Open all year. Eight rooms in main inn, sharing three baths, and eleven cottages, all with private baths. Rates: $60 to $180, including full breakfast. Children limited to cottages; smoking allowed in cottages and outside; French and Spanish spoken; no pets; Visa/MasterCard. Hot tub and sauna available to Creekside cottages. Horseback riding, kayaking, golf, whale watching, mushroom hunting, and beachcombing nearby. St. Orres recommended for dining.

DIRECTIONS: two miles north of Gualala on Hwy. 1.

A bird's eye view of the inn's dramatic setting overlooking the ocean beach.

PHOTOGRAPHS COURTESY WHALE WATCH INN

WHALE WATCH INN

Gray whale vantage point

At the Whale Watch Inn, natural beauty and refreshing salt sea breezes vanquish the stress and tension of everyday life. The inn is a complex of contemporary buildings designed so that every room

commands a sweeping view of the southern Mendocino coastline. Besides the vistas, the flicker of firelight in each guest's room creates a romantic atmosphere in the cool of the evening.

If guests desire to remain in a private world of their own, breakfast is delivered to the door each morning. Saturday evenings from 5 to 7 guests are invited to the hexagonal Whale Watch Room for champagne, wine, and hors d'oeuvres.

The weather pattern along this patch of coast is atypical. Known as "the banana belt," the Gualala area is free from the thick fogs that frequently blanket much of the northern coast of California. The result is an unparalleled vantage point on the pathway of the migrating gray whales that travel along the coast from winter to spring.

WHALE WATCH INN BY THE SEA, 35100 Highway 1, Gualala, CA 95445; (707) 884-3667, (800) 942-5342; Jim and Kazuko Popplewell, owners; Joanna Wuelfing, manager. Eighteen rooms in five contemporary buildings, each with private bath, 5 with full kitchens, all with fireplaces and private decks, 8 with double whirlpool tubs. Rates: $170 to $265. Includes full breakfast of fresh fruits, fresh breads, hot entrée delivered to the room. Visa/MasterCard/American Express. Private stairs to sheltered beach.

DIRECTIONS: from San Francisco take US-101 to Petaluma and proceed west through Two Rock and Valley Ford to Bodega Bay. Follow Hwy 1 north to Whale Watch at Anchor Bay, 5 miles north of Gualala.

The elaborate bed was used in the movie Wuthering Heights.

THE OLD MILANO HOTEL

Spectacular views of the ocean

Built in 1905 near cliff-hanging railroad tracks, this old hotel offers spectacular views. Though no longer part of the scene, the railroad is remembered. The owners have bought a caboose, placed it in their woods, and furnished it to perfection for the railfan. Formerly used by the North Pacific Coast Railroad, it has a guest suite for two, with kitchenette and observation cupola.

The hotel's six grand guest rooms overlook the ocean, and are furnished with antique armoires and curious beds, including an oak sleigh bed. Pale green floral William Morris wallpaper distinguishes the lavish, plushly furnished formal parlor. Stones collected from local beaches were used to make a large fireplace in an adjacent parlor, where wine from the hotel's extensive collection of Northern California wines is served in the evenings.

An additional option for guests is the white clapboard Passion Vine Cottage, located on the hotel grounds. Covered in salmon-colored passion flowers, it is fitted with a sleeping loft, sitting room, and small kitchen.

THE OLD MILANO HOTEL, 38300 Highway 1, Gualala, CA 95445; (707) 884-3256; Leslie Linsheid, owner. Nine rooms, including a Caboose, a cottage, and remarkable suite with a private sitting room overlooking the ocean. Private and shared baths. Open all year. Rates: $80 to $165. Includes full breakfast daily. No children; no pets; no smoking in the house. Visa/MasterCard. Hot tub. Massages available by certified practitioner. Excellent dining in restaurant on premises.

DIRECTIONS: on Rte. 1 one mile north of Gualala; the entrance to the hotel is on the left.

A unique guest room.

The Garden Room.

The Briar Rose Room.

GLENDEVEN

A north coast classic

A long-established inn, Glendeven is comprised of several handsome buildings on a two-and-a-half-acre headland just north of Van Damme State Park. The main inn is an 1867 New England-style farmhouse painted in subdued grey with white trim. The former hay loft has been converted into a lovely art gallery with an immense suite upstairs. Stevenscroft is a newer annex which houses four suites, all with individual fireplaces. A central water tower links this triangle of structures together.

The ten bedrooms and suites are spacious, uncluttered, and tastefully furnished with a blend of country antiques, contemporary pieces, and simple patchwork quilts. Some rooms, such as Briar Rose and The Garret, have dramatically pitched ceilings, and many rooms overlook the surrounding meadows. The

Left, the farmhouse that became one of the most popular B&Bs on the north coast.

Barn House Suite, which is sometimes used for seminars and corporate retreats, is so huge that it covers two whole floors, with two bedrooms, a living and dining room, kitchen and deck.

Owner Jan (pronounced "Yawn") de Vries, a Dutch-born craftsman, did most of the restoration work himself. He also designs and builds his own furniture, some of which is displayed in the Gallery at Glendeven. The gallery, which represents mostly Northwestern artists, contains a beautiful collection of paintings, crafts, and jewelry.

In the farmhouse kitchen, guests can help themselves to a cookie jar and refreshments, or wine in the afternoon. In the morning, you can have breakfast delivered to your room or join other guests in the living-dining room.

GLENDEVEN INN, 8221 N. Highway 1, Little River, CA 95456; (707) 937-0083; Fax (707) 937-6108; Jan & Janet de Vries, owners. Open all year. Nine rooms and Barn Suite, all with private baths. Rates: $70 to $275, including full breakfast and afternoon wine. Children welcome in Barn House Suite; no smoking; no pets; Visa/MasterCard/American Express. Hiking, canoeing, bicycling, botanical gardens, and downtown Mendocino nearby. Little River Restaurant, Cafe Beaujolais, and Albion River Inn recommended for dining.

DIRECTIONS: on Hwy. 1, just south of Mendocino and 1/4 mile north of Van Damme State Park.

Profuse flower gardens dominate the landscape.

MENDOCINO FARMHOUSE

The comforts of the last century

Down a dirt road far from noise and distraction, Mendocino Farmhouse lies in a clearing tucked into a forest of redwoods and firs. Marge and Bud Kamb built their tan two-story peaked roof farmhouse in 1975, drawing on their childhood memories of old houses. "We wanted high ceilings, paned windows, a swing on the porch," says Marge. The house successfully draws its guests into the comforts of the previous century.

The three bedrooms in the house, named for the Kambs' children, exude hominess. Karen's Room focuses on the antique white iron-and-brass bed, dressed with a Laura Ashley cream-on-cream moiré down comforter. The pine headboard and seaman's chest take center-stage in John's Room. Jim's Room features a rocker and woodstove, and a vista that encompasses a fish pond and its visiting duck.

The new barn cottage has two rooms with stone fireplaces: the Pine Room, sunny and close by the Secret Garden, and the Cedar Room, rustic, with cedar paneling and the intimacy of the forest.

The view on approaching, however, is a horticulturist's dream: white picket fence, two white arbors, and an English country garden filled with such evocatively named flowers as Canterbury bells, sweet Williams, and candy tufts. Marge doubles as a floral designer, using her garden, its roses, and the natural bounty of the woods for source material. The inn benefits with swelling bouquets spread throughout the house and fresh berries (in season) on the breakfast table.

The care Marge puts into her gardens is evident in her breakfasts as well—eggs come from resident chickens, fresh herbs spice the egg dishes, and all the jams are homemade.

MENDOCINO FARMHOUSE BED AND BREAKFAST. P.O. Box 247, Mendocino, CA 95460; (707) 937-0241, (800) 475-1536; **Marge and Bud Kamb, owners. Five rooms, all with private baths, four with fireplaces. Rates: $75 to $95. Includes full breakfast. Children and pets by arrangement; no smoking indoors; Sidney, a gentle golden retriever, and the cats Tinker, Bubba, and Oona are in residence; Visa/MasterCard. Good restaurants, hiking, canoe rentals nearby.**

DIRECTIONS: from Hwy. 1, turn onto the Comptche-Ukiah Rd. just outside of Mendocino. Go 1½ miles to Olson Lane, where you'll see a small sign. Turn left. The house is almost at end of road on the right.

Hosts Jim and Arlene Moorehead.

JOSHUA GRINDLE INN

A pioneer Mendocino inn

Visitors flock to the well-preserved old whaling town of Mendocino, searching for a bit of New England in northern California. No one can look at those fabulous ocean headlands without dreaming about leaving their rat race and retreating here permanently.

Jim and Arlene Moorehead, proud new owners of the Joshua Grindle Inn, did just that. In 1989, they decided to "chuck the corporate world" in the Bay Area, and acquired ownership of Mendocino's first small inn, furnishings and all.

The fine antiques and paintings in this fresh white house are distinctly early-American, in keeping with the New England heritage of its first owner, Joshua Grindle. He came out here from Maine in the 1870s to make his fortune in the booming lumber business, and his house remained in the hands of the Grindle family for nearly one-hundred years.

All five bedrooms in the main building are lovely, but of particular note is the Library Room, which features a four-poster bed, a woodburning fireplace with hand-decorated tiles depicting Aesop's fables, and a floor-to-ceiling bookcase enhanced by an antique typewriter.

Since opening its doors in 1978, the inn has expanded. A two-room, cabin-like cottage has been added to the grounds, and three bedrooms have been built inside their thirty-foot water tower. The "Watertower II" room is especially popular for its private treehouse feeling, up amid the one-hundred-year-old cypresses.

Guests may make their own breakfast selections from a buffet of juice, coffee, muffins, fresh fruit, and an ever-changing main dish such as tomato-basil frittatas or baked pears with yogurt (for which Jim and Arlene won a cooking award). This ample repast is eaten at a long pine harvest table dating from the 1830s. A short walk down the knoll to Mendocino is the customary way to work it off.

JOSHUA GRINDLE INN, P.O. Box 647, Mendocino, CA 95460; (707) 937-4143, (800) 474-6353; Jim and Arlene Moorehead, owners. Open all year. Ten rooms with private baths. Rates: $90 to $135 double, including full breakfast. No pets; no smoking; Visa/MasterCard.

DIRECTIONS: ask for directions when making reservations.

The Mezzanine Suite.

RACHEL'S INN

Set in a natural wonderland

Directly across the highway from Glendeven is Rachel's Inn, a mauve-colored, 1860s home which was once the area's first post office. Renovated in the 1980s, it contains a spacious dining room, upstairs sitting room, and five guest rooms, all of which overlook either the gardens, meadows, or coastal headlands. Decorated with a mix of old and new furnishings, each bedroom is painted a different color. The more luxurious Garden Room has its own entrance and a tastefully-appointed sitting room with upright piano and fireplace.

Adjacent to the Main House is the newly-built Barn which houses two bedrooms and two suites. The overall look here is more contemporary, with light pastels accenting each room. The Mezzanine Suite and Upper Suite both feature additional queen

Left, the garden is an important part of the inn.

wallbeds, wet-bars, refrigerators, and sitting rooms.

Rachel serves a lavish breakfast in the dining room, beginning with fruit, yogurt, and two kinds of bread. Her entrées range from eggs with mushroom sauce and asparagus, to pancakes, to scrambled eggs with pesto, to polenta with eggplant sauce.

The most remarkable feature of Rachel's, however, is the surrounding landscape. The inn is bordered by gardens, old cypress trees, and lovely Van Damme State Park. From here, lush trails wind out to the majestic cliffs overlooking the ocean and down to the beach, as well. Rachel, an environmental activist who is passionate about preserving the Mendocino coastline from offshore drilling, always encourages her guests to stroll through the park and absorb its natural beauty.

RACHEL'S INN, PO Box 134, Mendocino, CA 95460; (707) 937-0088; Rachel Binah, owner. Open all year. Nine rooms, all with private baths and most with working fireplaces. Rates: $96 to $185, including full breakfast. Children welcome; no smoking allowed in common room; no pets; no credit cards. Van Damme State Park, beach, Mendocino village, botanical gardens, Skunk Train, and whale watching (in season) nearby. Cafe Beaujolais, The Albion River Inn, and The Restaurant recommended for dining.

DIRECTIONS: on Hwy. 1, just north of Van Damme State Park and 2 miles south of Mendocino.

BREWERY GULCH INN

An enchanted garden

Legend has it that the omnipresent Mendocino fog always stops at the gates of the Brewery Gulch Inn. Whether or not this is true, the garden inside these gates is undeniably enchanted. The soft green lawn is covered with pines, creeping passion flowers, and more than twenty varieties of sweet-smelling roses. Whimsical bird houses hang from tree branches, and scads of hummingbirds hover over huge beds of fuchsias.

Built in 1854 by teamster Homer Barton and his sidekick, Indian Joe, the Brewery Gulch Inn is the oldest ranch in Mendocino County. Barton ferried his farm vegetables across the Big River every day, then later added a dairy and brewery. One of the original brewing stills now rests in the apple orchard.

Though just one mile from Mendocino, the inn has a rural feel. Five guest rooms, all with appealing garden views, are unpretentiously furnished. There are no keys to the rooms or house, and here, you will not feel the need for one. Guests have free use of the kitchen with its old wood burning stove.

Beyond the garden is the "Chicken Hilton"—a coop that is so charmingly constructed it is sometimes mistaken for a guest cottage. Built tongue-in-cheek by owner Arthur Ciancutti, the coop flaunts an undulating roof and cut glass windows. Little seed bags are even placed in your room with a sign that says, "For Your Chicken Feeding Pleasure." At least ten different sizes and colors of eggs are collected daily, and served for a hearty bacon and eggs breakfast.

The biggest decision to be made here is whether to feed the chickens or play a game of horseshoes. Guests like to stroll through the two-acre garden, play with Rolf (the Inn's springer spaniel, who earns his keep by chasing flower-eating deer out of the garden), and watch the fog roll into the nearby hay fields. But, notice how it never passes through the gates!

BREWERY GULCH INN, 9350 Pacific Coast Highway (Rte. 1), Mendocino, CA 95460; (707) 937-4752; Arthur Ciancutti, M.D., owner. Open all year. Five rooms, 3 with private baths, 2 sharing, 2 with fireplaces. Rates: $85 to $130 per room, including full country breakfast with fresh eggs from chickens on property. No facilities for children; no pets; no smoking indoors; Visa/MasterCard. Good restaurants in Mendocino and area. Whale watching in Nov. and March.

DIRECTIONS: one mile south of Mendocino at the water tower across from Smuggler's Cove.

THE STANFORD INN BY THE SEA

A Mendocino magnet

The Stanford Inn by the Sea is more than just an inn: Scattered across the ten acres of Mendocino riverfront land are also a California certified organic nursery, canoe and mountain bike shop, some eight resident llamas, fourteen cats, numerous horses, dogs, and black swans. All of these elements seem to co-exist peacefully and with the utmost environmental consciousness. Everything is recycled; the dried flowers from the nursery are made into wreaths for the inn; fresh produce from the garden is used for breakfast; whatever is left goes into a compost pile.

Though the setting is rural, the accommodations are far from rustic. Housed in a long, two-story lodge, all of the bedrooms have fireplaces, ocean-view balconies, local artwork against cozy wood paneling, four-poster or sleigh beds, and sitting areas with inviting velvet loveseats. Each room also comes

The inn and extensive grounds.

The indoor swimming pool.

Fiffler Sticks, the llama, is one of 8.

equipped with a stereo, VCR, telephone, welcome split of wine, and robes. In the lobby, cake is served in the afternoon, while the evening unfolds with wine and hor d'oeuvres. Guests wishing to work off the inn's hearty breakfast can slip into the lap pool, which is enclosed by a gigantic greenhouse-like structure.

The two visionaries behind this multifaceted compound are Jeff and Joan Stanford, the kind of couple who seem to thrive on managing five projects at once. Jeff is particularly enthusiastic about their nursery and loves explaining how everything is grown. Guests can take classes in organic gardening, medicinal herbs, and even yoga here.

THE STANFORD INN BY THE SEA, Highway One & Comptche-Ukiah Rd., PO Box 487, Mendocino, CA 95460; (800) 331-8884; (707) 937-5616; Fax (707) 937-0305; Joan & Jeff Stanford, owners. Open all year. Twenty-three rooms and six suites, all with private baths. Rates: $175 to $275, including full breakfast. Children welcome; no smoking; French, Japanese, and Spanish spoken; pets welcome; all credit cards accepted. Swimming pool, sauna, and hot tub on premises. Canoe, kayak, in-line skating, and mountain bike rentals available. Organic gardening, medicinal herb, and yoga classes can be arranged. Cafe Beaujolais, Little River Restaurant, and 955 Ukiah Street recommended for dining.

DIRECTIONS: on Hwy. 1 at Comptche-Ukiah Rd. just south of Mendocino village.

The swimming pool.

The mineral bath tubs accommodate most guests.

VICHY HOT SPRINGS

Uniquely healing waters

As the only naturally carbonated warm mineral springs in North America, Vichy Hot Springs has drawn visitors for a very long time. The source of the spring, which is still intact today, was once an ancient healing ground for the Pomo Indians. After the "Champagne Baths," or concrete mineral springs tubs, were built in 1860, Vichy Springs flourished as a summertime resort for many years until it fell into gradual disrepair. When current owners Marjorie and Gilbert Ashoff took over the spa, they painstakingly transformed it into a lovely bed-and-breakfast resort.

Today, instead of the likes of Mark Twain and Jack London, Vichy Hot Springs has become a retreat for movie executives, rock groups, and those seeking its effervescent, healing waters. Surrounded by seven hundred acres of natural terrain, the guest quarters—

Left above, the inn and grounds. Below, Gilbert and Marjorie Ashoff.

a long 1860s building and two 1854 cottages—are set around an expansive, tree-shaded lawn. The simple, cheerful bedrooms have retained some original touches, such as wood floors, original tubs, and concrete showers.

Across the lawn is an Olympic-sized swimming pool, while a short walk down a gravel path and over an arched Giverny-like bridge brings you to the massage building and mineral baths. The original concrete tubs, both outdoors and indoors, are ingeniously designed—just one pull of the stopper lets in the fresh spring water. After a blissful soak and massage, some guests barely make it back to their rooms.

VICHY HOT SPRINGS RESORT, 2605 Vichy Springs Rd., Ukiah, CA 95482; (707) 462-9515; Fax (707) 462-9516; Marjorie & Gilbert Ashoff, owners. Open all year. Fourteen rooms and cottages, all with private baths. Rates: $89 to $165, including full buffet breakfast. Children welcome; smoking allowed outside only; Spanish spoken; no pets; all credit cards accepted. Swimming pool, mineral baths (bathing suits required), hot tub, massages, facials, playground, and 700 acres of hiking and mountain bike trails on premises. Redwoods, wineries, Lake Mendocino, and museums nearby. Thai Cafe, North State Cafe, Angelo's Italian, and ElAzteca Mexican recommended for dining.

DIRECTIONS: from US-101, exit at Vichy Springs Rd. and follow historic landmark signs 3 mi. east to Vichy Springs.

The ranch, with the ocean in the background.

HOWARD CREEK RANCH

Rural retreat on the ocean

Bordered by the vast Pacific Ocean and set in a secluded valley surrounded by lush green farm country, Howard Creek Ranch is perfect for those who cannot decide whether to vacation in the country or stop by the sea. The main complex here comprises two back-to-back New England-style farmhouses furnished in true country fashion, with a fireplace, overstuffed furniture, and the unexpected—like a moose head over the piano.

HOWARD CREEK RANCH, P.O. Box 121, Westport, CA 95488; (707) 964-6725, Fax: use same no.; Charles and Sally Lasselle-Griggs, owners. German, Dutch, French, Italian spoken. Four rooms in main house, 3 with private baths and one sharing, plus a cabin converted from a boat, a cabin with skylights and an ocean view, and a rustic cabin. Rates: $55 to $145. Includes a hearty ranch breakfast of hotcakes, eggs, bacon, or sausage. Children often welcome by previous arrangement; Visa/MasterCard/American Express. Hot tub and sauna on side of mountain with great views. German massage by reservation. Forty acres of mountains, beaches, and pastures. Horse and carriage rides on site with two black percherons.

DIRECTIONS: located on Rte. 1, three miles north of Westport. Entrance is by milepost 80.49. Turn east and bear left and you'll see big white farmhouse.

One of the guest rooms has a private balcony. With a loft bed under a skylight, the other guest room looks out on the stars.

For those who like to rough it, there's the hull of a fishing boat that has somehow grown into a cabin complete with a galley kitchen, patchwork-quilt-covered bed, and a large picture window overlooking the creek. For those even more adventurous, another rustic cabin provides cold running water and a wood-burning stove.

Howard Creek Ranch provides the opportunity for beachcombing, swimming in a fresh-water creek, and bike riding along the beach—all offered up with country-style hospitality.

Many of the guests enjoy horseback riding along the beach or up through the hills while others relax on the lawn and keep an eye out for the blue heron and other species of birds.

A guest room.

THE HOTEL CARTER

An unimpeachable sense of style

PHOTOGRAPH BY DOUG PLUMMER

Guests are always asking Mark and Christi, "When did you restore this building?" Modeled after the original Cairo Hotel in Eureka's Old Town, the gracious yellow-and-white Hotel Carter is a newly constructed building that blends the elegance and ambiance of an earlier era with the comforts and conveniences of today. Old-world marble fireplaces and fourteen-foot-high ceilings dominate the lobby and dining room, where a compact-disc player and contemporary paintings by Humboldt County artists add a fresh sophistication to the space.

Besides showcasing local art, the Carters take pride in regional wines that they set out each evening. Dinner is served daily except on Tuesdays and, despite its relative youth, the hotel's restaurant has already been discovered by *Bon Apetit*. Small wonder, considering such sophisticated offerings as grilled quail salad with sautéed shitaké mushrooms, or an entrée consisting of sautéed marinated duck with apple-rasperberry gingersauce, toasted pecan-apple cornbread stuffing, beets, string beans, baby carrots, and purée of butternut squash.

Further enhancing their reputation for providing quality accommodations, the Carters traveled to England to search for the antique pine furniture that distinguishes the twenty guest rooms, all adorned with linens of peach and white. Wardrobes hide remote-controlled televisions, and eight of the rooms reveal soothing whirlpool baths.

THE HOTEL CARTER, 301 L Street, Eureka, CA 95501; (707) 444-8062, Fax (707) 444-8067; Mark and Christi Carter, owners. Twenty-three rooms, all with private baths, including 2 fireplace suites and 12 rooms with whirlpool baths. Rates: $125 to $225 double; includes a full breakfast and evening wine and hors d'oeuvres hour. Corporate rates available. Children are welcome; no pets; smoking okay by the lobby fireplace only; all major credit cards.

DIRECTIONS: take US-101 into North Eureka. Turn onto L Street going north. The hotel is on the corner of L and Third Streets.

STEVEN SIMMONS © 1988

Every hotel needs a lobby—this one is exquisite.

Left, the striking redwood exterior at night. Above, a deluxe guest room.

THE CARTER HOUSE

Re-creation of an earthquake casualty

Mark Carter found his dream house in a book of Victorian architecture at a friend's antiques store. The original house in San Francisco, destroyed in the earthquake of 1906, had been designed in 1884 by Samuel and Joseph Newson, who were also the architects of Eureka's famous Carson Mansion. Using the Newson's plans, Mark, with the help of several young assistants, re-created the house a century later. It took him sixteen months to complete his masterpiece of modern-day craftsmanship.

Extraordinarily fine antiques grace the parlors and dining room, but unlike Victorian homes, it has no dark or somber interior. White walls and marble floors blend with natural polished oak and redwood wainscoting, making all of the rooms bright and open. Contemporary paintings and graphics by local artists hang throughout the house. These, along with porcelain and ceramic pieces, are for sale in the Carters' first-floor art gallery. Woven baskets filled with potted mums are everywhere.

Breakfasts are supervised by Christi Carter, who formerly owned a restaurant and ice cream parlor. Pear, Grand Marnier, and almond filo tarts are not beyond her delectable repertoire.

Hospitality comes easily to the Carters, who serve cocktails and hors d'oeuvres in the evening, and cordials, tea, and cookies as a late-night snack. They are delighted to tell you about nearby Old Town, which is an impressive restoration of the surrounding waterfront, and to share with you their enthusiasm for the splendors of Eureka, of which they are so prominently a part.

THE CARTER HOUSE. Third & L Streets, Eureka, CA 95501; (707) 445-1390; Mark and Christi Carter, hosts. Seven rooms, all with private baths. Wheelchair access to one ground floor room. Rates $125 to $225. Includes an elegant, full breakfast of fresh fruit, an egg dish, muffins, and delicate pastries. Wine and cheese in the late afternoon, sweets in the evening. Business rates mid-week. No children or pets; no smoking; all major credit cards.

DIRECTIONS: take US-101 into North Eureka and go west on L Street.

The decorative rear parlor personifies the Victorian ideal.

AN ELEGANT VICTORIAN MANSION

A total Victorian experience

In a town full of historic buildings (nearly 1,600, in fact), this inn stands out as one of the finest examples of Eastlake cottage-style architecture along the West Coast. Though it looks like a mansion, the structure is classified as a "cottage" because of its one-and-a-half stories, two flanking bay windows, and ornate bargeboards that festoon the gables.

William S. Clark, twice the mayor of Eureka, lived here for over fifty years. Because his family figured prominently in Eureka's history (and literally owned half the town), Clark entertained many famous guests, such as Lily Langtry and Ulysses S. Grant, at his home during the turn of the century.

After one hundred years of private ownership, the home was turned into a bed and breakfast in the 1980s. Its name is derived from its 1888 newspaper description—"An elegant Victorian mansion." Present owners Doug and Lily Vieyra, a spirited couple, love "playing" their roles to the hilt. They also operate The Chalet de France, an unusual Swiss-style mountain retreat, complete with Tyrolean costumes. The motto for their inn is, "Come to where history lives." Doug says, "We want to relive that exciting transition period from the horse to the automobile." They greet their guests in vintage costumes, and enjoy staging mystery weekends, classical concerts, and guided tours of Eureka in antique cars.

Guests enjoy a total Victorian experience, drinking old fashioned ice cream sodas on the veranda of an afternoon, walking in the Victorian flower garden, watching silent films in the evenings, and taking tours of Eureka in antique automobiles. Even if the

Victorian ambience overflows into the Edwardian era, guests don't mind at all.

Inside the mansion itself, elaborate ceilings, painted chandelier medallions, wall coverings by Bradbury & Bradbury, and carved fireplaces enhance the original splendor of the two parlors, dining room, and library. An enclosed porch wraps around the back of the house, where a Finnish sauna is concealed. (Belgian-born Lily also offers Swedish massages.) A formal garden of over one-hundred roses beckons guests to step outside, and go back to a gentler era of croquet and afternoon tea.

AN ELEGANT VICTORIAN MANSION, 1406 C St., Eureka, CA 95501; (707) 444-3144 or 442-5594; Doug and Lily Vieyra, owners. Open all year. Four rooms, 2 with private baths and 2 sharing 3 baths. Rates: $85 single, $100 to $145 double, including full gourmet breakfast. Children over 15 welcome; no pets; no smoking; Dutch, French, German spoken. Interesting variety of cuisine served in area, from continental, Mexican, Chinese, Italian, to seafood and logging camp food. Croquet on grounds. Eureka offers tennis, beach combing, watersports, fishing, ocean charters, theater, opera, classical music concerts, night clubs.

DIRECTIONS: from south on US-101, at Eureka turn right at stop light onto Wabash for 9 blocks and left onto C St. for 3 blocks to inn on left at 14th St. corner. From north US-101 becomes 4th St. Go through town to C St. and turn left at Denny's for 10 blocks to corner of 14th St.

Ornate Victorian gingerbread decorates the exterior of the house.

GINGERBREAD MANSION

Everything adds to the fantasy

A spectacular peach and yellow high-Victorian, the Gingerbread Mansion has delicate woodwork around turrets, gables, tower, and porches. Two camellia bushes, shaped into trees, stand guard in front of the house and add to the fantasy. Called the "Butterfat Palaces of Cream City," houses like this one were built for Ferndale's successful dairy farmers. It is situated only one block from the shops, restaurants, and live theater found on Main Street in Ferndale, a historic town nestled against the foothills of the redwoods.

Ken Torbert bought the mansion in 1982 and turned it into an extravagant bed and breakfast. It now extends to eleven large, antique-filled guestrooms and suites, four parlors, and a formal dining room. Each guest room has a private bath, and the Fountain Suite has side-by-side claw-footed tubs for "his and her" baths, and a chaise lounge in front of the fireplace.

The furnishings are eclectic. Pieces include Victorian settees, Eastlake tables, and carved French armoires, as well as a variety of patterned wallpapers, a bird's-eye maple fireplace, Oriental carpets, and wood-burning Franklin stoves.

Little extras add personal warmth to the elegance. Turned-down beds, bathrobes, early-morning coffee or tea, vintage bicycles for exploring back roads leading into nearby canyons, and boots and umbrellas if it rains are amenities appreciated by guests who stop here.

THE GINGERBREAD MANSION, 400 Berding Street, Ferndale, CA 95536; (707) 786-4000; Ken and Sandie Torbert, hosts. Eleven large, elegant guest rooms, all with private baths. Rates: $140 to $350. Includes a generous homemade full breakfast and full afternoon tea. No pets; no smoking permitted. Ferndale is a designated state historic landmark town. Visa/MasterCard/American Express.

DIRECTIONS: from US-101, exit at Ferndale. Proceed about five miles into town and turn left onto Brown Street at the Bank of America. The house is ahead on the left one block.

SHAW HOUSE INN

Original Victorian Carpenter Gothic

Completed in 1866 for Seth Lewis Shaw, the founder of Ferndale, this house has endured as a remarkable contribution to the historical integrity of the area. The elaborate Victorian Gothic Revival house of steep gables, recessed porches, intricate gingerbread trim, and balconies is set along the creek that Shaw first navigated into this valley. Built on land he cleared of overgrown ferns, the house is a tribute to his pioneering spirit.

Norma and Ken Bessingpas, the new owners, have furnished the house with care. There is a mixture of old and traditional in the parlor—original floral turn-of-the-century wallpapers in mauves, pinks, and greens, a Victorian swan-necked cream-colored couch, hooked rugs, old baskets, antique lighting fixtures, and wonderful pieces of china. A walnut paneled library with floral patterned chairs offers up old books, a viewer, cards, and games.

The bedrooms, decked out in floral wallpapers, have sloped ceilings, mauve carpeting, oak furniture, and Laura Ashley quilts. Three of the rooms have private balconies overlooking the well-kept park-like Victorian gardens abloom with old wisteria bushes, roses, hydrangeas, rhododendrons, fuchsia, nasturtium, and holly. Woodpeckers, thrushes, warblers, and egrets have found a home here.

The hosts provide a walking tour map and bicycles are available for riding around this charming Victorian town of 1,300 people, all of whom take great pride in keeping up their homes and gardens. Luscious flowers are everywhere, and Russ Park on the edge of town is a popular sanctuary for birds. The ocean is just four miles distant.

SHAW HOUSE INN, 703 Main Street, Ferndale, CA 95536; (707) 786-9958, (800) 557-7429, Fax (707) 786-9958; Norma and Ken Bessingpas, owners. Six rooms, all with private baths. Rates: $75 to $135. Includes continental plus breakfast of fresh fruit, egg dish, homemade bread and Victorian specialties. Children over nine welcome; no pets; smoking on outside balconies and porches; Visa/MasterCard/American Express.

DIRECTIONS: from US-101, exit at Ferndale. Proceed about 5 miles and the sign for Shaw House is on the right.

The view of the cove from the inn is fascinating because the weather is constantly changing.

TRINIDAD BED BREAKFAST

Beachcombers' delight

The view of the harbor is unforgettable from this Cape Cod home 175 feet above the quiet cove of Trinidad Bay. A sleepy village of about 400 people, Trinidad has a winter fishing fleet of seventeen boats that anchor here. In summertime the number increases to over 300 boats and yachts bobbing in the cove. They are protected from the ocean swells, often twenty and thirty feet high, by a jetty of land known as Trinidad Head.

While exploring nearby trails around Trinidad Head, walkers end up at the most westerly point of land in California, where whales and otters are easily spotted. On one side the ocean crashes against the rocky coastline, on the other side lies a calm, protected bay. A favorite excursion along an old stagecoach road leads down to Indian Beach where beachcombers delight in the driftwood that washes ashore. The two major redwood national parks, a thirty minute drive in either direction, makes this location ideal for outdoor buffs.

Innkeepers Carol and Paul Kirk couldn't be more hospitable. Having raised a family and toiled in the corporate world, they settled quite happily into this rural community. Early in the morning Paul might be glimpsed in his overalls en route to oversee their family run restaurant. Carol might already be kneading dough for the morning meal. Rockers by the brick fireplace on an enclosed porch and attractively decorated guest rooms with magnificent views make this a particularly wonderful place to be. Whether the fog is rolling in or the sun is shining, the ever changing scene enhanced by the distant clang of buoy bells is magical.

TRINIDAD BED & BREAKFAST, 560 Edwards Street, P.O. Box 849, Trinidad, CA 95570; (707) 677-0840; Carol and Paul Kirk, hosts. Four ocean-view rooms, all with private baths, two are suites, with private entrance and breakfast delivered. Rates: $105 to $155. Mid-week rates available. Includes hearty breakfast of fruits, warm breads, muffins, and local cheeses. Extraordinary view of Trinidad Bay. No pets; no small children; smoking outside only; Visa/MasterCard/Discover; personal checks accepted.

DIRECTIONS: from the south on US-101, exit at Trinidad and follow Main Street through town. With the bay straight ahead, the inn is on the left.

Left, a great place to view the Pacific Ocean. Above, the Beluga Whale Room.

THE LOST WHALE INN B & B

Spectacular

Set on a cliff above perhaps the most stunning stretch of coastline in California, The Lost Whale Inn is a spectacular retreat. Far below, the waves crash against jutting rocks where hundreds of sea lions bask.

The Cape-Cod style inn is light and airy, with amber Douglas fir floors and high, angled ceilings. Even on cold winter days, the Great Room stays warm and cheery with its wood-burning stove and panoramic windows.

Susanne Lakin, an artist, and Lee Miller, a musician, came to Trinidad several years ago, and fell in love with these four acres of pine-covered land. They built the two-story home as a bed and breakfast inn ("We got the design from a Mozart record jacket."), and opened in 1989. Susanne has an adjoining art gallery, and many of her silkscreens and paintings hang throughout the inn.

The Lost Whale Inn is equally fun for families and romantic couples. Children may romp in a custom-built playhouse; feed the resident goats, bunnies, and cats; and explore the tidepools without disturbing other guests. Three of the six bedrooms have lofts for children, and walls are sound-insulated. The only set ritual is an easygoing, more-than-you-can-eat breakfast, at which everyone sits together.

THE LOST WHALE INN B & B, 3452 Patrick's Point Drive, Trinidad, CA 95570; (707) 677-3425, (800) 677-7859; Susanne Lakin, Lee Miller, innkeepers. Open all year. Eight rooms, all with private baths, 2 have balconies, 3 have lofts, 5 have ocean views. Rates: $95 to $125 double, less $10 single; extra adult $15, child 3–16 $10. Mid-week winter discounts. Includes full country breakfast and afternoon tea. Children encouraged; no pets; smoking outside only; Visa/MasterCard. Play house and farm animals for children.

DIRECTIONS: 4 miles north of Trinidad on Patrick's Point Drive (call for directions).

BED AND BREAKFAST ASSOCATIONS

CALIFORNIA ASSOCIATION OF BED AND BREAKFAST INNKEEP-
ERS, 2715 Porter Street, Soquel, CA 95073; (408) 464-
8159, Fax (408) 462-0402. *Serving the entire state with
262 members.*

BED AND BREAKFAST INNKEEPERS OF NORTHERN CALIFORNIA:
P.O. Box 7150,,Chico, CA 95927; (800) 248-INNS. *Serving northern California.*

BED AND BREAKFAST INNKEEPERS OF SOUTHERN CALIFORNIA.
Box 1818, Idyllwild, CA 92349; (909) 659-3202. Co-
ordintor, Diana Dugan. *Serving Southern California.*

THE INNS OF POINT REYES, P.O. Box 145, Inverness, CA
94937; (415) 663-1420. (Free brochure available).

BED & BREAKFAST INNKEEPERS OF SANTA CRUZ, P.O. Box
464, Santa Cruz, CA 95061-0464; (408) 425-8212.
(Free brochure available).

WINE COUNTRY INNS OF SONOMA COUNTY, P.O. Box 51-B,
Geyserville, CA 95441; (707) 433-INNS. (Free
brochure available).

GOLD COUNTRY INNS OF TUOLUMNE COUNTY, P.O. Box 462,
Sonora, CA 95370; (209) 533-1845. *Represents 14
places.*

SACRAMENTO INNKEEPERS ASSOCIATION, 2209 Capitol Avenue, Sacramento, CA 95816; (916) 441-3214. (Free
brochure available).

RESERVATION AGENCIES

ACCOMMODATIONS IN SANTA BARBARA, 118 Nopalitos Way,
Santa Barbara, CA 93101; (805) 882-1300. Buck But-
ler, manger. Call from 8 A.M. to 6 P.M. *Santa Barbara
and area from Oxnard to Cambria.*

AMERICAN FAMILY INN/BED AND BREAKFAST SAN FRANCISCO,
P.O. Box 420009, San Francisco, CA 94142; (415) 931-
3083; Richard and Susan Kreibich. Call Monday to Friday 9:30 A.M. to 5 P.M. *Private residences and luxurious
yachts. San Francisco, Marin County, Carmel/Monterey,
the Wine Country.*

BED AND BREAKFAST EXCHANGE, 1458 Lincoln Avenue #3,
Calistoga, CA 94515; (707) 942-5900. *Cottages and
small inns in the Napa and Sonoma wine country, San
Francisco and northern coast.*

BED AND BREAKFAST EXCHANGE OF MARIN, 45 Entrata, San
Anselmo, CA 94960; (415) 485-1971; Suellen Lamorte.
Around-the-clock. *Homestays, small inns, and private
cottages throughout Marin County.*

BED AND BREAKFAST HOMESTAY, P.O. Box 326, Cambria, CA
93428; 805-927-4613; Jack and Ginny Anderson. Call
any time. *Ocean views and secluded custom-built homes.
Hearst Castle area and California central coastal re-
gion.*

BED AND BREAKFAST INTERNATIONAL, P.O. Box 282910, San
Francisco, CA 94128-2910; (415) 696-1690, Sharene
Walsh. 8:30 A.M. to 5 P.M. weekdays; 9 A.M. to noon on
Saturdays. *Private homes, apartments, houseboats, and
inns. California, Hawaii, Las Vegas.*

EYE OPENERS BED & BREAKFAST RESERVATIONS, Box 694, Al-
tadena, CA 91001; (213) 684-4428 or (818) 797-2055.
Ruth Judkins and Elizabeth Cox. 9 A.M. to 6 P.M. *Private
homes and bed and breakfast inns throughout California.*

MEGAN'S FRIENDS BED AND BREAKFAST RESERVATION SERVICE,
1776 Royal Way, San Luis Obispo, CA 93405; (805)
544-4406; Joyce and Robert Segor. *Cambria, Los Osos,
San Luis Obispo, Pismo Beach, Paso Robles, Solvang,
Baywood Park.*

WINE COUNTRY BED AND BREAKFAST, P.O. Box 3211, Santa
Rosa, CA 95403; (707) 578-1661. Helga Poulsen. *Wine
country and Northern California.*

WINE COUNTRY RESERVATIONS, P.O. Box 5059, Napa, CA
94581-009; (707) 257-7757.